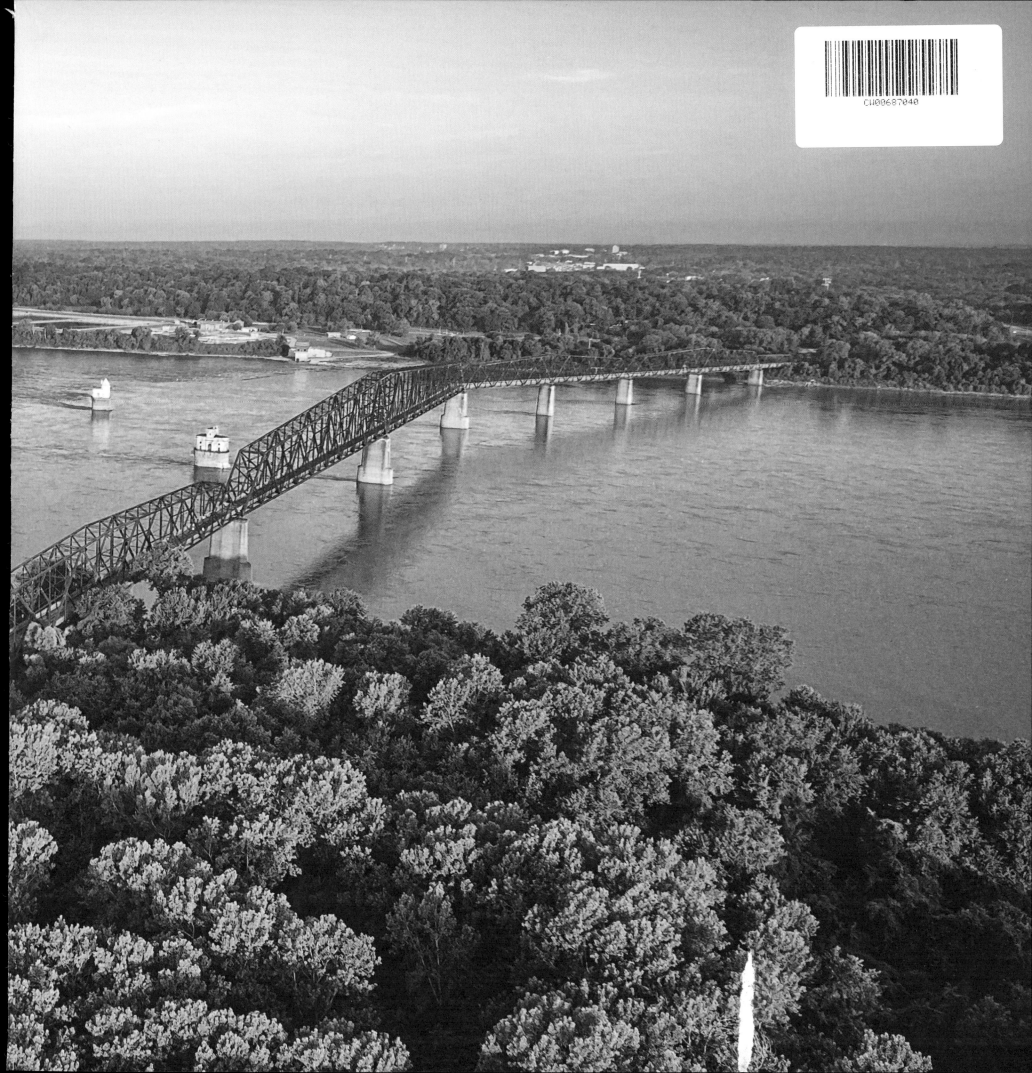

To Alan & Sue

The Great River Rowed

The Mississippi Million

With my grateful thanks for you kindness, support and friendship!

JOHN PRITCHARD

NAPIER PUBLISHING

A man's reach should exceed his grasp...

Robert Browning

Acknowledgements	8
Map	9
Foreword	10
Introduction	12
Stage One: **Lake Itasca to Minneapolis**	24
Stage Two: **Minneapolis to St Louis**	74
Stage Three: **St Louis to Memphis**	128
Stage Four: **Memphis to New Orleans**	174
Epilogue	240
Participants	250
Index	252
Picture Credits	256

Acknowledgements

The Mississippi Million Team On and Off the Road:
Paddy & Mel Broughton, Alex Conty,
Jeremy Dale, Peter Gate, David Keane,
Magenta McDougall, Graeme & Gillian Mulcahy,
Charlie Pritchard, John Pritchard

The Mississippi Million Team Support:
Donna De Stefano, Anna Gray

The Mississippi Million Participants (Rowers & Coxes):
Dan Adams, Kevin Arnold, Tom Barry, Matt Brittin,
Paddy & Mel Broughton, Stuart Chase, Marysh &
Alison Chmiel, Mike & Kate Colling, Jeremy Dale, Will
Docker, David Ellis, Kelly Ennis, Jim Eyre, Kyra Felisky,
Chris Gate, Freddie Gate, Maeve Gillespie, Stephen
Gillespie, Charlie Green, Kate Hampton, Simon Hotchin,
Simon Holden, Lucy Horgan, Matt Horgan, Jeffrey
Hughes, Simon Irish, Johann Koss, Mark Machin, Sosefin
Malowkski, Derek Mayne, Graeme & Gillian Mulcahy,
Magenta MacDougall, Jayne Pasternak, Michael
Pasternak, Stephen Peel, Jim Pew, Charlie Pritchard,
Jerry Rees, Repton Salisbury, Gavin Sayers, Charles &
Pamela Schroeder, Richard Stow, John Taylor, Andy
Trahar, Mark Vickers, Rachel Vickers, Steven Webber,
James & Olivia Whitworth, Dalayne Williamson, Harry
Williamson, Julie Williamson, Mark Wilson, Simon
Woods, Sarkis Zeronian

Right To Play (USA & UK): Meryl Davies, Michael Evans,
Johann Koss, Sharon Petrie, John Pritchard, Carin Zaleski

Events in USA: Dan & Trish Adams, Sean Kennedy,
Carin Zaleski

Stanley & Thomas Boatbuilders: Julian Perry,
Mark Stanley

The Skiff Club: Roger Haines, Fran Kenden &
The Skiff Club Committee

The Brains Trust (Physiology): Courtney Kipps,
Juliette Lloyd, Justin Roberts, Robert Shave,
Paul Thawley

Allium (Event organiser): Rachel Dulai,
Will Glendinning, Sarah Rule

Health & Safety (Capita): Jeff Protheroe,
Martin Suzan, Eleanor Western

Boat transporter: Cii

Mississippi Million Sponsors: General Mills,
Goldman Sachs Gives, Karwoski & Courage,
Kirkland & Ellis LLP, Larson King, Mazda,
Oceanwood Capital, Target

Editor: Jo Russell

Design: Bobby Birchall, Bobby&Co

DEDICATION
This book, and indeed the entire project, would
have been impossible without the support and
wise guidance of my wife, Julie Williamson.
Also, the inspiration for the project stemmed from
the wonderful Richmond Chirrapah. This book is
dedicated to them both.

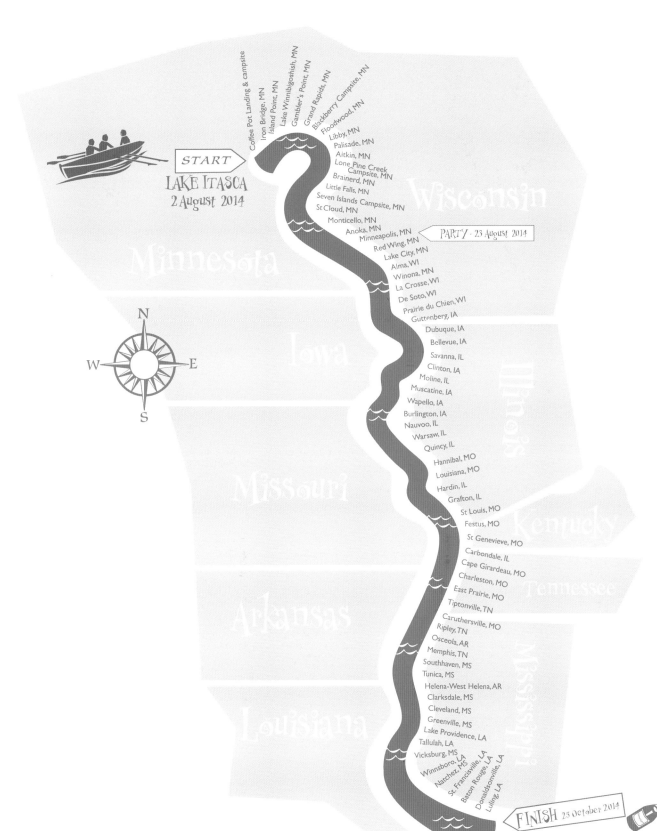

START
LAKE ITASCA
2 August 2014

Coffee Pot Landing & campsite
Iron Bridge, MN
Island Point, MN
Lake Winnibigoshish, MN
Gambler's Point, MN
Grand Rapids, MN
Blackberry Campsite, MN
Floodwood, MN
Libby, MN
Palisade, MN
Aitkin, MN
Lone Pine Creek Campsite, MN
Brainerd, MN
Little Falls, MN
Seven Islands Campsite, MN
St Cloud, MN
Monticello, MN
Anoka, MN
Minneapolis, MN
Red Wing, MN
Lake City, MN
Alma, WI
Winona, MN
La Crosse, WI
De Soto, WI
Prairie du Chien, WI
Guttenberg, IA
Dubuque, IA
Bellevue, IA
Savanna, IL
Clinton, IA
Moline, IL
Muscatine, IA
Wapello, IA
Burlington, IA
Nauvoo, IL
Warsaw, IL
Quincy, IL
Hannibal, MO
Louisiana, MO
Hardin, IL
Grafton, IL
St Louis, MO
Festus, MO
St Genevieve, MO
Carbondale, IL
Cape Girardeau, MO
Charleston, MO
East Prairie, MO
Tiptonville, TN
Caruthersville, MO
Ripley, TN
Osceola, AR
Memphis, TN
Southhaven, MS
Tunica, MS
Helena-West Helena, AR
Clarksdale, MS
Cleveland, MS
Greenville, MS
Lake Providence, LA
Tallulah, LA
Vicksburg, MS
Winnsboro, LA
Natchez, MS
St. Francisville, LA
Baton Rouge, LA
Donaldsonville, LA
Luling, LA

Minnesota

Wisconsin

PARTY - 23 August 2014

Iowa

Illinois

Missouri

Kentucky

Tennessee

Arkansas

Mississippi

Louisiana

FINISH 25 October 2014

NEW ORLEANS PARTY!

N
W E
S

Foreword

John Pritchard called me one day saying, 'Johann, we are going to row the Mississippi River for Right To Play.' I vividly remember thinking that it was a crazy idea and secretly hoping that he would not ask me to join him… 'And you will do it with us,' he continued. I had not been in a rowing boat since I was seven and taking three months off to row was not in my plans. I was doubtful that his idea would even work, but did not want to stifle his enthusiasm. 'Okay…', I replied, uncertainly. 'And we will raise one million dollars for you!', he said. That changed things. When someone as accomplished as John declares something like that, the only response is, 'YES! Fantastic!'

Thankfully, John conceded that I only need join him for a couple of days, and we were both glad that I was not in a boat for longer. The first day we rowed together, not only was I heavy and uncoordinated, but my every stroke was in opposition to his. Fortunately, the second day was a bit better.

John performed a miracle on the Mississippi River. With each day, and every stroke, he moved closer to his goal of rowing the entire river in an old Victorian boat. Moreover, with each day he was closer to the one million dollar target. John and the team had their struggles, their laughs, many visiting rowers, thousands of stories, and the ability to execute a task never previously achieved. Their success inspired thousands of kids around the world in our programs, raised more than the promised million dollars, and generated support and awareness all over the world.

This is the story as it unfolded, and I am extremely grateful to have been a part of it. The enthusiasm and the vision that preceded the adventure, and the determination to reach the goal, comprise an inspiring story for us all. It is a story I want to tell my children. There are so many people who say something is impossible and that we should not care. John cares and he makes the impossible possible.

THANK YOU from all of the children benefitting from your efforts.

Johann Koss
Founder, Right To Play

Introduction

Introduction

There's an old joke that goes, 'What's the difference between eggs and bacon? It's the difference between involved and committed – the chicken is involved, but the pig is committed.'

The moment we loaded two Thames skiffs onto a container to be transported to the American Midwest for the start of a 2,320-mile row, there was the sense that all those of us involved in the Mississippi Million challenge had just become pigs.

The aim was to row 2,320 miles from Lake Itasca in northern Minnesota down to New Orleans in Louisiana over three months, rowing essentially a marathon per day, at a pace of around 4mph. It would be a gruelling physical activity that, in terms of physical energy expended, meant I would still lose 40 pounds even if I managed to eat over 5,000 calories a day. To make the journey just a little spikier, the row would be in Victorian Thames skiffs, made of African mahogany and English oak, the design of which is essentially unchanged after two hundred years or more. These boats give no credence to modern-day attributes such as sliding seats, energy-efficient outriggers, and sleek narrow shells made of ultralight carbon Kevlar.

But they are beautiful. They have been captured in paintings by Canaletto, Whistler, Wylie and others who were captivated by river scenes, and rightly so. Their elegance and design make them absolutely belong on and to the river. Besides their beauty, I loved the idea of an eccentric middle-aged Englishman rowing the length of the most iconic river in North America in a Victorian wooden boat with fixed seat and fixed pins. To my knowledge, no one had done it before, although there was possibly good reason for that.

The idea was mad, but not totally off-the-scale bonkers. I was, after all, a rower, having rowed in two Olympics as well as several World and

European Championships. And I would not be alone. I would have around fifty intrepid and slightly deranged friends joining me. Top of that list was Paddy Broughton, a fellow rower from my days at Cambridge, who had agreed to give up three months of his life to row the entire length with me.

There were plenty of areas of concern, not least my backside. I was now in my mid-fifties, and more used to the office-based day job than spending hours upon hours rocking backwards and forwards on a wooden seat in a

boat. Even with sheepskin pads, I had already developed two nasty lesions right under my rocker bones in the practice sessions before we even hit the Mississippi.

I had also been warned, gleefully, by any number of different folk about the difficulties I would face. These included, but were not limited to, snakes, snapping turtles, alligators and jumping Asian carp. Also add to this list of possible horrors, ticks, black fly, leeches, horseflies, hornets and of course the mosquito. These Jonahs would inevitably add, after reeling off this list

of merciless and voracious consumers of my flesh, 'of course, the river is beautiful though...'

Despite this list, one of the things that held real fear for me was an unquestionable villain in its malevolence and ability to drain the spirit and will: the plain old-fashioned wind. This was especially true in its most unwelcome form, the headwind. I had studied the Mississippi, its course and its climate history, and a few things had become clear. Firstly, as the river snakes this way and that all the way to the Gulf of Mexico, the wind would feel like it was coming from all directions, but I guarantee the only one worth noticing would be the headwind. Rowing into a headwind saps both mental and physical energy, as you feel like no matter how hard you

Left and above:
The official launch party.
Giving joy rides to
the supporters.

try, you are being pushed backwards and effectively making no progress. Secondly, from time to time, this wind could cause serious standing waves, especially on some of the lakes we would cross or where the river is at its widest. These could easily be sinking conditions. And this was just the regular 20mph-or-more wind, not a tornado, which I had been told by cheery folk are common to the point of unremarkable. But the thing I feared most, to the point of dread, was the lower Mississippi. This section comprises longer stretches of open and fairly straight courses, and I worried about finding myself confronted by a relentless headwind through whole days and weeks when I was already weakened. There were no tools or devices to combat this enemy other than small technical adjustments, brute force and a complete bloody-minded will to persevere.

Whether I would be able to prevail through the long days that beckoned was one of the questions I was apprehensive about answering and was the reason I adopted a mantra for the project, borrowed from my friend Derek Mayne who uses it when scaling high mountains such as Manaslu, an 8,000-metre peak in Western Nepal: 'I have the absolute right to go as slowly as I want. But I do not have the right to stop.'

The reason I did not have that right was simple: too much was at stake.

Which brings me to the reason for taking on the Great River. I first became involved with the charity Right To Play (RTP) in 2009, and I had travelled to Africa, with my wife Julie and son Charlie, to see first-hand the work that they do. Put succinctly, the charity uses the act of play, in all its forms, as the vehicle by which to educate, empower and protect children in the most disadvantaged countries in the world, living in some of the harshest conditions, whether in communities facing extreme poverty or refugee camps set up in war-torn regions. These camps house ex-child soldiers – children aged ten who have no posters of sports or pop stars on their walls, but instead have images of martyrs. Many of these children's sole aspiration is to die like these martyrs. At least until RTP helps them to see there are other ways to live and thrive.

We visited one school in Ghana for children with learning and physical disabilities. It was truly humbling. In a society where there are a lot of

Above: Charlie Pritchard, a figure of some interest to the children in the RTP programmes.

Above: Children will often walk several miles to and from school to take part in the RTP programmes.

Above: The 'Jumping Beans'. These children, not much more than toddlers, were SO excited to see us they did not stop bouncing during our visit.

plantains to pick, if you can't pick plantains then plan B is not attractive. There is nowhere else for these children to turn; the school is the one hope for them.

I was playing with the kids when I noticed Richmond. He was the same age as Charlie, but half his size. He has Down's syndrome and was too small to play with the big kids, but he was clearly something of a character. He was bouncing around like a little jumping bean. He started playing with my digital camera and then came back, climbed on my lap, and just held me for nearly half an hour. That sense of need and humanity was incredible. The teachers later told me that their biggest problem is depression. There just aren't enough staff to give these kids – who are essentially abandoned by their parents – the TLC they really need.

Back at the hotel that night, I gave Charlie a hug. Then it struck me, and I said to him, 'Who's hugging Richmond tonight, like I'm hugging you? And who's going to hug him tomorrow night? And the next night?'

It was at that point I decided to do something that would move the needle. I would row the length of the Mississippi in a boat called Richmond. I would tell everyone his story, and by so doing, I would raise $1m for Right To Play, which would have a truly significant impact on the lives of thousands of children like Richmond who essentially have less than nothing.

It is one thing to decide on such madness, quite another to put the plan into action. Enter stage left my wife, Julie. She is a girl of the Midwest, born in Iowa City, Iowa, and has lived in the UK for over twenty years. She lived with me plotting this madness for three years before turning around and saying, 'Listen, row the damn river or stop talking about it.' Or words to that effect – evidently, I underestimated her command of Anglo-Saxon.

Being the woman she is, she didn't then stand back and watch me flounder and fail, but gave me all the help, guidance, encouragement and positive criticism that was required to bring all the elements together. She even learned to row from scratch. She is steadfast, indefatigable, tenacious,

Above: The RTP directors with the teachers at our first school visit.

Above: The moment my life changed – one long hug from Richmond and the Mississippi project was born.

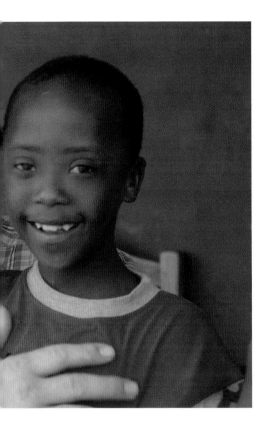

Above: The main man, Richmond Chirrapah.

horribly smart, and in short, the quiet architect of all that is good in my life. I have little doubt that had I known her thirty years ago, my Olympic silver medal would have been gold.

Without Julie, this project would not have got off the ground, and I wouldn't have found myself standing by a large container, watching two skiffs being sealed up, destination the American Midwest.

Stage One
Lake Itasca to Minneapolis

Some facts about the Mississippi River. It is the second-longest river in the US, often called the country's spine, flowing 2,350 miles from its source at Lake Itasca to the Gulf of Mexico. When linked with one of its tributaries, the Missouri River, it is the fourth-longest in the world. At its widest, it stretches over eleven miles from one side to the other. In short, it is immense. It is also a major industrial waterway, with 60 per cent of US grain exports carried along on huge barges capable of carrying the equivalent of sixty tractor-trailers' worth of produce. And we were going to tackle it in two Victorian skiffs. Given our paltry size in comparison to its might, it seemed fitting to bestow on this great river the moniker 'The Dragon' – a being capable of roaring and causing mayhem with one flick of its tail, and one that warranted respect.

But for all the grandiose talk, at its source the Mississippi is a tiddler. For the first 125 miles, it would be too narrow for our majestic skiffs and we would be in two Grumman aluminium canoes. Rowing in one would be Paddy accompanied by a guest rower, with me and a guest rower in the other. In large part, this would be the format for the trip. While Paddy and I would be the constants, we would be joined by guest participants, who would row with us for two days at a time, and who had committed to raising significant sums of money for Right To Play simply for the pleasure of doing so. As we would be facing backwards while rowing, we would also each have a steerer. This, amongst other things, had made the planning of the trip a Herculean task. Stopping points had had to be charted, hotels and campsites booked, support-vehicle routes mapped, food, drink and essential supplies contemplated. On top of this we now had to ensure that we would be at the right exit points, notwithstanding weather conditions or other boat calamities, to meet up with the next plucky participants for every one of the planned eighty-four days on the river.

Right: A clear view of the complex and serpentine Mississippi.

Left and opposite:
The moment of truth –
opening the container
to check if the skiffs
were matchwood!

The fact that Paddy would be alongside me every pull of the way was of huge comfort. He is a character straight out of H. Rider Haggard's books, an adventurer whose first instinct is to smile and laugh.

I first met Paddy in 1984. I was in a meeting room at one of the more beautiful Cambridge colleges with a large group of oarsmen, gathered to hear the plans for the assault on Oxford and the Boat Race in spring 1985. There were coaches, boatmen, old faces from the previous year's campaign, and several new faces on top of a variety of bodies for us old lags to assess. One of these was a fresh-faced, big block of a lad called Patrick Broughton – or, as we all soon knew him, Paddy.

Most of the other newcomers were ex-schoolboy rowers and there didn't seem to be an ounce of grit amongst them. But Paddy stood out – and not just because he was six feet five (rowing has lots of tall people). There was a steel about him and it was quickly clear he had the ability to be a catalyst in a group. This was a critical, natural element of Paddy that was apparent not just during his distinguished rowing career, but also throughout his life and career.

He has always been his own man and marched to his own beat, which is always the sign of someone comfortable in their own skin. After Cambridge and a few successful years in the City, he stepped back, bought a sail boat and sailed to Australia. He took his time but, having reached Oz, he stayed, then set about another successful career and married the brilliant Mel.

When I told him about the Mississippi project, its scale, duration, objectives and the absolute certainty of hideous pain and suffering over a protracted period, his email reply was short: 'I'm in.' When I asked for how much or how long, the reply was equally short: 'The lot.'

Lake Itasca – 3 August 2014

Day one. The talk was over and the challenge was on. To get to the very top of the Mississippi and fire the gun for the start of our 2,320-mile odyssey, we had to paddle across a section of Lake Itasca towards a man-made dam and the post – yes, the post – that marks the beginning of this great river. It was a gentle warm-up paddle across still clear water, but already we could see what might lie ahead. The trip was as much a punt as a paddle, as we negotiated through thick reeds to reach our large wooden pole.

With us was Julie, who had flown from London for the weekend to be head cheerleader, my father-in-law (aged eighty-four and were proving that age is but a number) as the first of our guest rowers, my sister-in-law and my niece. I was, I regret to say, a little short with people who were all trying to help me. How could they not understand that I just wanted to start? Three years of pondering and one year of intense planning had come down to this moment and I wanted to be off!

Above: An inaugural launch of the skiffs on Lake Itasca.

Above: Paddy, me, Mark Wilson and our (ever-present) mascot, Harry Williamson.

Above: Paddling our canoes in preparation for the start of the journey. Harry, aged 84, leading the way.

After many, many ceremonial photos, we were on our way, spirits high but with a little trepidation. This first day was to be a very gentle introduction to the river, covering a mere sixteen miles through gently flowing streams and in glorious countryside, but spiced up by some modest rapids. It turned out, very quickly, to be a much, much harder proposition than any of us had imagined.

For a start, it took us some time before we were able to row. The first stretch was little more than a ditch, involving more dragging and pushing than paddling. We were soon into wetlands through which meandered a very small stream. The water was on the low end of normal, which meant we were running into rocks, sunken logs, sandbanks and gravel beds. We were using a guide that had been compiled by the Army Corps of Engineers (ACE). It pointed out that, unless there is a fairly decent amount of flow, you can get very lost here.

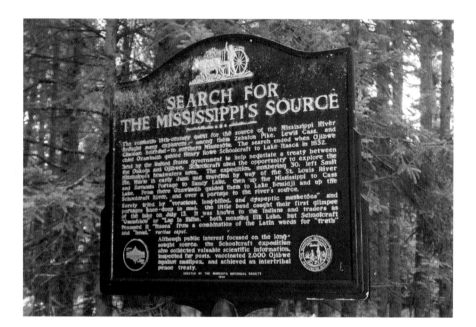

Left: Ground Zero – the source notice in Itasca.

Right: And so we begin…

The guidebook was not the only harbinger of doom. After several hours of rowing and dodging rocks we bumped into a couple of guys poling their canoes upstream to catch minnows in order to fish for the famous Minnesota walleye (a form of pike). They were very friendly but looked like they were straight from central casting – bearded, untroubled by teeth and wearing clothes that were strangers to the laundry room. They had recently seen Julie and regaled her with stories of people dying on the river, stuck up to the neck in Mississippi mud and perishing horribly. They advised her, reassuringly, that if we didn't have enough stream and tried to get out we could drown in the mud and never be seen again. My mind drifted back to the days before we had left for this epic adventure, and Julie, amongst myriad other tasks, sorting out the completion of our wills. 'Just good

housekeeping, darling – read nothing into it,' she had cheerily said.

Thankfully, there was enough water to prevent us disappearing without trace, although sadly not enough to float us down some of the inappropriately named 'rapids'. The lack of water necessitated getting in and out of the canoes and hauling them manually over each and every obstacle. Imagine an aquatic version of the Field Gun competition at the Royal Tournament, except that instead of lasting two minutes and forty seconds, it lasted nine hours.

We finished the sixteen miles at 6 p.m., making it a very, very tough introduction. Any idea that we would be masters of this river was dispelled immediately, not by huge expanses of water, biblical rains and tornadoes or commercial traffic, but by sixteen miles of dark woods with swirling streams containing slippery, ankle-breaking stones. From day one we could see that we should never, ever take this river for granted.

After sleeping the sleep of the dead in a tent, we set off the next day to be met by superb weather and unbelievable beauty, with bald eagles

Above: Me, Julie and Charlie stretched across the mighty Mississippi.

Above: Very difficult early miles…

and other creatures everywhere. The landscape, however, continued to pose challenges. Downstream from our campsite, the ACE guide helpfully noted: *'Caution: The Mississippi enters a large wetland and finding the channel can be a challenge in low water conditions.'*

Yes, indeed. Neither Paddy nor I are short men, but with reeds the same height as us when standing up in the canoe, it was incredibly difficult to spot the right path. Particularly when that channel is no more than three feet wide.

However, once we had negotiated safe passage through the reeds, the Mississippi showed us another side and we positively flew down the river, this time managing twenty-six miles in seven hours, finishing feeling fresh and recharged for the next day. So far, it had been a game of two halves, as the egregious commentators are wont to say.

Right: Note how (too often!) the river winds back on itself – heartbreaking.

Left: Navigation was not easy…

Wild at Heart

In this first spell of five days, during which we travelled from Itasca over 120 miles to Leech Lake, we began to glimpse some of the majesty of this river. There is ludicrously beautiful scenery along with spectacular birds and wildlife (not to mention the vegetation by the riverbank – displays of water lilies that would make Monet weep).

One day, one of the team saw two grey timber wolves standing in the road – bold as brass – staring straight back at them. At this point, they decided that the appropriate response was orderly retreat. Not long after, we spotted what looked like a white tail crossing some distance behind us – a deer? On closer study, the specimen in question looked slightly different – darker, moving differently and, although it must have been a large stag or buck, it had no antlers. It then, and only then, dawned on me that this was no deer, but a mature black bear. Here's the thing: as a child from a council estate in Fulham, I might have seen the odd deer in nearby Richmond Park, but the sight of a bear gave a certain pause. Once I spotted it, it is fair to say that our speed picked up significantly until my heart returned to something near normal.

But this was just the large animals. It was the small creatures of the forest that brought the sense of quiet and charm that bestowed a tranquillity on any who saw them. Most of us on the team were city dwellers, so finding ourselves in this towering, green cathedral, constructed over countless millennia, brought an almost spiritual sense of belonging and respect. We were all instinctively aware that we were in someone else's backyard now.

The bald eagles were almost comically magisterial, with that penetrating visage that looks permanently irritated that you are near them, coupled with an almost haughty indifference. Then there were the lightning-fast kingfishers that zipped in and out of their nests buried deep into the banks of the river. At first, one's eye barely caught them, such was their speed.

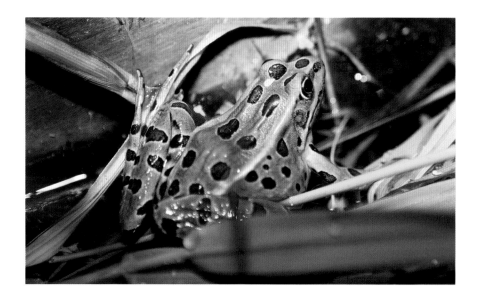

Right: Early signs of (benign!) wildlife.

Then, as one's sight adjusted, the kaleidoscopic colour variations started to become more apparent as they swooped and darted. In these early days, we all felt clumsy and alien in this bucolic setting, but we were hopefully beginning to feel as if we belonged.

Alongside its majesty, we began to see small suggestions of the truly awe-inspiring power of the river. We travelled through rapids and gravel beds that span us sideways with a flick of the stream. We jigged this way and that through dark forests of sunken trees; we hit submerged stumps and were thrown into the river many times from our sturdy canoes. At times it felt like we were picked up and moved thirty feet sideways by some invisible hand. This contributed to our belief that the Mississippi was a sleeping dragon. So far it had been benign, with just the occasional flick of its tail to remind us it was there, waiting. Above all, it *demanded* respect.

The 100-mile Mark

Day six was an opportunity to give it the respect it deserved. We were to row fourteen miles across Lake Winnibigoshish, which translates as 'troubled shallow water'. This was not a great sign, especially as the lake looked more like a sea.

We turned to the ACE guide, which again helpfully noted: 'High winds and boat washes make crossing the lake hazardous. Paddling across the lake is not recommended.' Anyone fool enough to try should go around the edge, it continued, or words to that effect.

We were rightly nervous and made all the preparations we could in case of emergencies. Other than going around the edge, obviously. With two strong paddlers accompanying Paddy and me in the canoes, we decided to go straight across.

Below: A becalmed Lake Winnibigoshish.

Below: Lucy and Matt Horgan lead the way. Paddy and I watch nervously.

Below: How can you not love Lucy!

We were reliant on the dragon being kind, and thankfully it was, with a gentle breeze of maybe 5mph. But even with this benevolence, it was tough going. Paddy likened it to doing a very long run on a treadmill: hard work and seriously boring as there's nothing to look at and a sense of getting nowhere. It took us about four hours, the first two hours spent anxiously scanning the skies for signs of bad weather, the last two with us growing in confidence that we could finish unscathed. Once we were in the middle, we realised that 10–15mph winds would have made the lake impassable for us and even potentially seriously dangerous. But with the dragon dormant, we survived, said goodbye to our canoes and got ready for the skiffs.

And as Paddy noted, somewhere on Lake Winnie we passed the 100-mile mark for the challenge. Only 2,220 to go.

A Closely Held Secret

When Julie and I go on a really good holiday, we feel almost proprietorial about the location. We want it to be ours and to keep it as our secret. We like to think of it as romantic – a way of preserving the moment and place just for us. So you will understand why I will keep the location of an astonishing family we met coming out of Lake Winnie under wraps. Nothing could have prepared us for this family's staggering generosity, starting with their insistence that we camp at their property by the banks of the Mississippi.

At this point, our support team had expanded to twelve people, plus three big tents, three huge vehicles, a boat trailer and a thirty-five-foot RV (campervan). 'No problem,' they said, looking at our cumbersome entourage. 'Plug that RV into our electricity. Please come in and use our shower. Need to cook? Here is a big cooking pot for your pasta. Let us build you a camp fire while you cook. Short of some sleeping mats? Here, use these. Mosquitos? Yes, use our stuff, it works better.'

Above: Base camp at the Bromenschenkels'.

Above: The caravanserai of the Mississippi Million.

Above: The gang, ready for our barbecue by the river.

The matriarch of the family has made a habit of scooping up itinerant paddlers as they come down the river (which flows beautifully by their garden) and she keeps in touch with their progress via Facebook. She is simply magnificent and is aided by her husband, who also loves the company, and their fabulous daughter, who is just about to go off to college.

As if their hospitality the night before was not enough, the following morning out they came with a huge stack of blueberry pancakes, bacon and home-made maple syrup. And all of this was done for complete strangers with no question of reward of any kind other than their company by their fire. Their attitude embodied the generosity of spirit that we were to encounter on so many occasions on our journey, and was an absolute joy.

So these generous people shall remain anonymous, but for the sake of argument we will call them Sandy, Jeff and Emma Bromenschenkel, at Deer River, Minnesota, right by the banks of the Mississippi. Don't tell anyone, but if you ever bump into them give them a *huge* hug because they are the best.

Flies, Damn Flies

Towards the beginning of our second week, we were travelling through gorgeous countryside, slipping along at 5mph. All was calm, tranquil and wonderful. Then we entered a wooded section, which was different but equally beautiful. But this beauty came at a price. We ran into biting flies. Not just a few, but clouds and clouds of biting horseflies, deer flies, mosquitos and chiggers. This was the biennial convention of biting insects, so everyone was there. And it was happy hour in the bar. We were bombarded, first being bitten on the hands, then arms, then under our legs

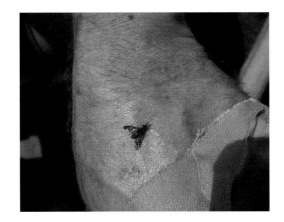

Right: The deer fly –
vicious, vigorous and
extremely attentive.

as we rowed. And then they got nasty – they went into our ears, up our noses and inside our sunglasses. I had been expecting some form of biting infestation – but this? We fought back by using Aussie napalm, a concoction that Paddy had brought along, and that slowed them a bit. And we learned a whole new art – skiffing while swatting.

The next day we set off, targeting thirty-four miles, and immediately ran into our old friends, the vicious deer flies. No mosquitos, I assume because they are simply too nice and friendly to compete for fresh meat and blood with these aggressive and predatory demons. After attacking every possible spare inch, the deer flies seemed to devise a particularly cunning and unwelcome strategy: biting us under our legs while we were rowing and thus could not swat them. They seemed to hover in clouds over eddies in the river, but swarmed over us when they smelled blood. The worst for me was being bitten on the forehead, the culprit having flown up my sunglasses, and also being bitten on the lip. Yuck. Paddy had wisely invested in a pair of long trousers, which was a good call.

The silver lining to the fly-infested cloud was that at the end of the day, we had the prospect of a stop in the Country Inn, Deerwood. After striking camp at 7 a.m. every day, sometimes in the rain, living in damp and smelly clothes (I didn't want to be near me, and over the last half-century I have got used to me!), sleeping on inflatable mattresses with lumpy foam pillows, and eating whatever we had from bowls that had been given a cursory rinse in cold water for the last eleven days, I had never looked forward to staying in a hotel as much as I yearned for the Country Inn, Deerwood.

It was a prospect that excited us all, not least Alex, our flamboyant physio. It was strongly suggested by those wiser than me that one of the key members of the team should be a physio, preferably with some expedition experience. Our medical contacts placed an ad (God knows where) and a shortlist of folk duly emerged. I met several, but one stood out and was immediately the front runner – step forward, Alex Conty.

Alex is a former French soldier, a physio, who is built like a muscular jockey (in fact, I think he may once have been a jockey) and has a deep love of camping and wilderness living. Most of all, and in common with everyone on the project, he was willing and able to take on any task. As we were to discover, unbidden, he would simply take on anything that required addressing: striking camp, driving the RV, finding a spot for river exits and – most crucially – repairing the many and various ailments of the visiting participants. These poor, willing, nervous folk often had hands that looked like butcher's shop windows and blisters in the most delicate of locations – Alex? No problem. Back strains, Alex? No problem.

He had a physio practice in London and was clearly putting down London roots. One aspect of this was that whilst his English was just fine, he was prone to occasional comedy malapropisms, especially when either agitated or fuelled by Maker's Mark bourbon, a happy weakness of his.

There was only one recurring issue – he had a slightly 'French' attitude to driving. This meant that he permanently drove 5–10mph too fast in any given situation, leading to some alarming braking. He also saw stop signs as an indication to speed up. In the sleepy Midwest and the even-sleepier South, these traits often led to full and frank exchanges with the locals and Paddy continually suggesting that Alex's parents were definitely not married when he was born.

Above: Alex Conty – The Blister King (not always on people's hands…!). Our ever smiling physio.

Opposite: The glory of the river and verdant bluffs.

Overleaf: Mark Vickers, me and Charlie Pritchard, with our full daily load.

The Shape of the River

In addition to attending to matters of personal hygiene, our first rest day in Deerwood gave me the opportunity to think about the route we had so far taken. It was remarkable how far we had rowed and yet what relatively little distance we had covered as the crow flies.

One of the features of this truly extraordinary river is its constant changing shape. While the ACE's highly detailed maps of the river are extremely useful, they are rendered inaccurate within a calendar year as the relentless power of the river erodes the banks in its continual pursuit of a straighter course.

When we started paddling in these beautiful wetlands, we meandered with the serpentine river, backwards and forwards, our views obscured by tall reeds and bulrushes. After a couple of hours' paddling, we would stand in the canoe in the hope of checking our course (it was surprisingly easy to follow a tributary only to find it a dead end). At that point we would discover that, although we had covered several miles of river travel, the actual distance as the crow flies was more like a mile. Although this was deflating, the novelty of being in an aquatic maze certainly made the travel intriguing.

In addition to the reeds, the nature of the riverbanks makes the life of trees that have grown by the water's edge highly precarious. As the river continues its insidious clawing at the banks, it drags sand and mud from the exposed roots of these trees. From time to time one will lose its grip on the land and slide into the river. As we were to learn, these sometimes huge cottonwoods, in full leaf, could be a constant floating menace. We all loved this section of the river, but it was pretty clear to us who was in control and had the greater might. And it was not us.

Deerwood also gave us the opportunity to tuck into what were to become two team staples – Sam Adams beer and chicken wings. Wings are

a perennial in the Midwest and appear on the menu of any self-respecting restauranteur. However, their appearance and taste could differ wildly. What makes a perfect wing is, of course, an intensely subjective matter and open to heated discussion, but the team was at least agreed on the following:

Size: matters. Bigger is generally better, but not if they look like steroidal East German wings.

Quality: the bones must be actual bones that could support the weight of a well-fed fowl. They must not be the porous, bendy, pathetically weak imitations of bones that you sometimes find.

Sauce: the most contested area. Dry rub versus wet? Buffalo versus BBQ or, heaven forfend, teriyaki or something equally ghastly.

Heat: even if there is unanimity on sauce, there is debate as to heat – mild in a way that would barely raise an eyebrow from someone raised solely on milk, through to lip-blisteringly intense.

Such cerebral debate would make the evenings to New Orleans fly by.

Winds and Rapids

Having flown along on our first day out of Deerwood, powered by an astonishing and welcome tailwind and a very strong, helpful stream, the prospect of a row of around twenty-six miles on the second day seemed easily within our grasp.

The river thought differently.

We had some factors that simply weighed against us. Firstly, we were rowing towards one of the dams on the river, so the flow that had carried us so well slowly diminished over the day to zero stream for the last ten miles. Secondly, the river became essentially a lake as it approached the dam, which sucked the life out of what little stream there was and also gave a greater area for the main enemy of the day – the wind. Our third issue, therefore, was that we were heading due south into a 10–12mph southerly wind. The net result was that, instead of easily rowing twenty-five miles in four hours as on the previous day, twenty-six miles took us nearly six hours – and that is six hours of deadlifts, twenty-two times per minute. I also made the stupid error of consuming insufficient food and water, so I 'hit the wall' with an hour to go. I was in bad shape at the end and almost inhale a sandwich and down two litres of water. Lesson learned.

The next day, we woke to find the headwind had moved on and we had a stunning forecast. We were excited for the day's row. We were aiming for thirty-two miles in three chunks, in hot weather and on a river like glass, which would be wonderful stuff. And sure enough, for the first eleven miles, we plodded through some gorgeous scenery. We stopped again with nine miles left to run, full of good humour and looking forward to tea and banana bread. Then it happened.

At first, we just saw eddies and bubbles on the water and noticed the stream getting faster. Then we started to notice that the river floor was getting perilously close to the boats. Then we saw them – rocks, and rocks

Above: Good technique. Paddy leading the way, me gratefully following.

mean rapids. We worked hard, really hard, to avoid them but inevitably we hit them and ran aground. The sound of those rocks hitting our beautiful boats was sickening to hear and we all jumped out and floated the boats gingerly to deeper water. The last nine miles were scary and draining.

We finished the day chastened by the experience, and looked with trepidation at the bottom of the boats. Thankfully, the sound had been worse than the outcome, with the steel keel band taking most of the impact. But once again the river had shown us just who was boss.

Ewaut

One of our great hopes of the trip was that we would encounter some of the true characters to be found along the length of the Mississippi. Our first may not have been home-grown, being a slightly 'unhinged' but hugely kind and entertaining Belgian, but was a character nonetheless. He was splendidly called Ewaut Van Wassenhove. We had seen him a few times, paddling his Grumman aluminium canoe solo, weighed down by all his gear but always smiling. We had learned that he was also heading to the Gulf and, having paddled past him previously, this time we happened to reach the end of our twenty-two-mile session just as he reached the same stopping point.

We helped him out of the water and offered him a sandwich and a drink. He was very grateful and sat happily chatting to us for a while. He was twenty-one, skinny as a rake, with a fabulous hat, safari shirt and trousers and a big pair of green wellies. You couldn't make it up. He told us he had started three months earlier in Ghent, hitchhiked to Cambridge and begun camping wherever he could. He went from there to Ireland and then to Canada for a while. He went to the source of the Mississippi, bought a canoe, paddle and some gear and set off for the Gulf. After New Orleans, he intended to head to Texas, then Arizona, and then down to South America before returning to Ghent. What an amazing adventure.

I asked him if he was staying in touch with his family and he said his biggest supporter was his dad, a fanatical aficionado of American jazz and part-time Lindy-hop dancer. His dad had given him some contacts in Burlington, Iowa and New Orleans.

I am a great believer in helping folk out as we go, as we may well run into times when we need help too, so I suggested we give our new friend a hand with his portage. Almost inevitably on untamed stretches of river, you encounter obstacles such as fallen trees or, more commonly, shallow rapids

Above: The irrepressible, indefatigable and wholly unique Ewaut

Above: Ewaut and his entire worldly possessions.

with rocks that will rip the bottom from a boat. Confronted by these, there is only one option – drag the boat from the water and carry, or portage, the boat past the obstacle to calmer, clear water.

Given the distances and the amount of gear he had, Ewaut's portage would have taken him all day. He was therefore delighted to accept our offer, and we duly took him before agreeing that we would look out for each other down the river. He said he would aim to get to New Orleans at the same sort of time as us. He then showed exactly why it is right to spread goodwill whenever you can: he said that, even if we didn't meet in New Orleans, he would sell his canoe and canoeing gear and put the money into the Mississippi Million. And all we gave him was a sandwich, a drink and a lift.

And into Minneapolis

When we began to properly plan this extravaganza, reaching New Orleans seemed an almost impossible task. The first, and symbolically important, achievement was to reach the Twin Cities (Minneapolis and Saint Paul). Julie and I were married in Minneapolis and so these two very different but equally wonderful cities are close to our hearts.

To help us on the two-day row in, we were joined by Johann Olav Koss, founder of Right To Play and much-medalled Olympian. He had a baptism of fire. We had to cover thirty-two miles due south, into a 10mph headwind, rowing the last five miles towards a dam and the consequent end of any helpful flow to speed our progress. That is to say, it was hard and got harder.

Below: With the great man, Johann Olav Koss.

Below: Me with Johann and a flag with our intentions clear.

Below: Graeme Mulcahy attempting to coach Johann. Johann has his own ideas…

We managed to negotiate some unexpected rocks at the beginning, some of which were the size of small cars, and we swung this way and that, terrified of destroying the boats.

We got through these rapids and then just kept pushing on, like the fish in *Finding Nemo* – just rowing, rowing, rowing. The headwind kept pushing us back, to the extent that we were barely making any forward progress. Mile after heavy mile we kept going until finally we could see the dam, which was our finish point. It had been seven hours of lifting, but we had made it. We were all pretty 'tuckered', as Paddy would say, but we had not faltered.

It was at this point, as I was congratulating Johann on his heroic effort, that he revealed this had been his third time in a boat. Ever.

Left: Me and Jeff, Paddy and Kelly in canoes to navigate shallow rapids.

Below left: Launching the skiffs from a soft sand bar.

Opposite top: An increasingly feral Paddy.

Opposite bottom: Harry, David Keane, JOK, Graeme, me, Jeff Hughes and Paddy – start of a good day.

Overleaf: All days should have been like this.

The following day we needed to row through the first three of many locks – Upper and Lower St Anthony's Falls and the deeply unromantically named Lock Number 1 – and from there on through Minneapolis, finishing at Saint Paul.

The locks form part of a huge engineering project, the aim of which was to retain the Mississippi as a commercial waterway. In the 1930s, the ACE began constructing the Upper Mississippi River and the Illinois Waterway 9-Foot Channel Project (nine feet being the required depth to offer reliably safe passageway for commercial traffic). Alongside dredging the channel, much of this was achieved through a system of locks and dams.

As the ACE explains, there are twenty-nine locks and dams running from Saint Paul to St Louis, with a drop of 420 feet in elevation. These dams form pools very similar to long narrow lakes behind them, making the river deep enough for large towboats to navigate. The locks then form a 'stairway for boats', raising or lowering them from one pool to the next as they go up or down the river. Once below St Louis, the river is sufficiently deep that there's no longer any need for locks and dams.

Above: JOK adds his considerable frame to the coxes' seat!

Above: JOK and me, full steam ahead.

Above: Entering the stupendously huge locks…

Overleaf: Paddy and I, coxed by Graeme, show how it should be done.

I was looking forward to experiencing the first of these locks, and obviously looking forward to the end point. But, as ever, it would not come easy.

The day we were to start our approach arrived with a bang. Biblical claps of thunder accompanied Hollywood-style lightning from 5 a.m. We were all shaken awake by the storm's power and peered nervously into the gloom to see the rain hammering down. We delayed our start by an hour to let it clear, which it duly did, but to give some perspective, the two and a half hours of rain deposited two feet of water in the skiff on the top of our trailer.

I was tired from the previous two days' headwind and was worried that I might be in for a sub-par day, the forecast being for another day of headwind. But the mantra of the project was apt: 'I have the right to go as slowly as I want, but not the right to stop.' The first five minutes were slow, but we soon began to find a pace that surprised me, and I shook off my doubts and leaned into the oars with unexpected relish.

What a day it turned out to be. The first twelve miles flew by and we reached the Upper St Anthony's Falls lock quickly. I have travelled through locks hundreds of times on the Thames, but nothing prepares you for the sheer scale of these Mississippi locks: the size of a small football pitch, accompanied by mechanical gear of gigantic proportions and surrounded by roaring waterfalls (imagine a smaller Niagara). They are so large, they have their own visitor centres and guided tours, not something you might find in Sunbury-on-Thames!

They are manned, invariably, by the nicest, funniest guys around, who joke and support in equal measure. The lock doors close and you descend five, then ten, then twenty feet, on and on until finally reaching fifty below your start. The two skiffs, filled with grinning fools, looked ridiculous in these vast tanks, but boy what a sight.

Three of these beauties marked our day. Johann climbed back into the bow seat and, inspired by his lessons the day before, found his form and rhythm and we flew over the last ten miles to our end point in Saint Paul. We were greeted by a small but perfectly formed group of friends and family. We were simply thrilled to have reached our goal and joyously drained the ice-cold Sam Adams beers that were presented to us.

Right: Paddy, Jeff, me and JOK on a well-earned break.

Stage Two
Minneapolis
to St Louis

Partying in Minneapolis

I knew that if we made it as far as Minneapolis, still in reasonable heart with most of the bits still intact on our inevitably weakened bodies, we would have taken a major step towards our distant goal. Reaching the dock at St. Paul Yacht Club, the sense of relief, achievement and elation was immediate – all emotions magnified by the presence of our merry band of supporters.

From the moment we got out of the boats, we were inundated with the indispensable Sam Adams, support, family, friends and more Sam Adams. For the rest of that evening and for the next two days, we were carried along on a tide of goodwill, with ever more friends appearing and the group consequently growing.

On the first evening, having scraped off days of Mississippi mud, sweat and a few tears, twenty of us repaired to a local bar, which proved to be huge fun.

We were set to continue our rating challenge of the best wings, when our eyes fell on one item on the menu that we could only assume had been included as a late April Fool joke: 'Waffles with Chicken'. In advance of its arrival, we speculated about what this culinary conundrum might actually be, for what it most definitely could *not* be was waffles with chicken. How wrong we were.

Up it came, a picture-perfect waffle, with two jugs, one containing warm maple syrup, the second containing something that looked like nuclear waste but was billed as sausage gravy. On top of the waffle was a piece of third-rate Kentucky-style fried chicken. Not only was there precious little edible flesh on this, but also it was coated in a layer of armour-plated breading. Johann jumped in, poured both jugs and tasted the combination, hoping against hope for culinary alchemy. The disappointment was palpable. He

Right: A beer cures most ills.

Below: 'Refuelling...'

Above: The Mississippi in Minneapolis, viewed from the Guthrie Theatre.

instantly pronounced it inedible and handed it around the table for others to try. A few brave souls stepped up to the plate and were left gagging. We were told that waffles and chicken is the dish *du jour* further south where we were heading. We could hardly wait...

That night I slept poorly, my mind unable to switch off from the enormity of the achievement of simply reaching here after years of dreaming, as well as what the next two days held. These were billed as rest days, but with friends, family and two receptions in the diary, they would be anything but.

The first official reception was the following evening. Over a hundred people gathered for drinks and canapés in support of the project and Right To Play generally, at the splendid Guthrie Theatre overlooking the river. Johann spoke brilliantly, and I said a few words. The response from the room was wonderful and the whole team felt a real sense of coming home.

Sunday morning saw us at the Minnesota Boat Club, paddling in the skiffs and taking out any of the rowers from the club who fancied trying their skills. It was a huge hit and I was on the water for three hours.

Above: The Guthrie
Theatre, our main
party venue.

We then had a second event on Raspberry Island, generously sponsored by Target and local firms Larson King and Karwoski & Courage, and we had a fabulous afternoon of barbecue, beers and music supplied by the brilliantly named Front Porch Swingin' Liquor Pigs, a local Minneapolis band. The turnout was fantastic. We had over 150 people there and, more importantly, raised more money for the project. We began to see that we were starting to build real momentum, with more and more people spreading the word and evangelising the cause. It really could be possible to achieve our objective of raising $1m. There were so many reasons why it was important – possibly 1,100,000 reasons, which is the number of children RTP help every week.

Earlier, I mentioned the story of Richmond, the disabled boy in Ghana whose humanity, humour and spirit inspired me to undertake this madness. But let me give you one other tale.

When you visit many parts of West Africa, you find different levels of infrastructure – some extremely poor, almost to the extent of non-existence, and some rather better, but all invariably shabby. In parts of

Ghana, there are lovely roads that just end and become red dirt paths into the bush. In other areas, basic provisions for the bare minimum of civilised existence are few and far between. Standpipes for clean water are a revelation. On our trip to Ghana, Julie and I met many children in our programmes. They were all inspirational in their own ways, but Julie got talking to one boy in particular and her conversation with him moved her in much the same way as did mine with Richmond. She was talking to him after the games had ended and asked him how long he had been in the programmes. 'About four years,' he replied. He was sixteen and came from a subsistence-farming family in the bush outside Accra. Until he had learned about things via RTP, he had simply expected, if he was lucky, to be a plantain farmer like his father. Now, he told Julie, he had many things he would like to do. 'What do you really want to do, then, when you leave the school and the RTP programmes?' she asked him. 'I want to be the man who finishes our roads,' he said.

Above left: Me in full flow at the party.

Above: The wonderful Carin Zaleski, RTP National Director, US.

Above: Me and JOK – a happy couple!

Above: Honours board at the Minnesota Boat Club – our wonderful hosts.

Top right: Graeme giving a skiffing 'taster'.

Right: Carla Colborn and Pat Courtmanche, who sang at our wedding in 1996, giving a reprise!

Overleaf: The very challenging launch ramp at the Minnesota Boat Club.

Back with a Bump

The one downside to our two magnificent days in Minneapolis was an almost complete lack of rest, and I feared that I would pay dearly over the coming days. My fears proved prescient.

We were to set off from St. Paul Yacht Club cheered on by our merry gaggle of friends and family. The unwelcome extra attendee was an extremely strong wind. What this translated into was very choppy water with white caps everywhere from the moment we set off. We were soon in the absolute thick of it, water blasting against the boats and just – only just

Below: Always the stars of the show: an admiring crowd for the skiffs.

Right: The 'Big Guns' – Paddy and Chris Gate, steered by Pamela Schroeder.

– failing to breach the gunnels. The amount of water sloshing around was exacerbated by the wash from industrial traffic slapping against the hard concrete walls constraining the river.

After managing 6–8mph on some stretches, we were down to 2–3mph and the wind grew ever stronger. There was no let-up, and it was just a matter of gritting teeth and pushing on.

We finally reached our overnight stop at 4 p.m., twenty-six miles and eight hours later, and I felt really beaten up by the conditions. Paddy had a twinge in his back, while Chris Gate, one of our fellow rowers, had some heroic blisters on his derrière to be treated. I just looked older.

Chris's blisters seemed poor recompense for his immense contribution to the Mississippi challenge. Some time previously, at the National Schools regatta in which both our sons had been racing, Chris had asked me how the Mississippi plans were going. I confessed that I was daunted by the scale of the target I had set myself as well as the length of the river. Chris, with his clear-eyed approach to life that is so endearing, simply said, 'JP, not only can you do this, but you *will* do this. Furthermore, it will be a huge success and I will help you all the way.' With that, he committed to buying the two boats, Richmond and Doreen, as well as contributing via his business. While the practical support was hugely welcome, it was the vote of confidence that made the world of difference.

Above left: Freddie Gate, our cox for the day, who didn't mention his private stash of pizza.

Right: A beautiful, winding stretch of river.

Above: Me, only 6' 3", next to Chris Gate…

Below: Welcome to the beautiful but deeply treacherous Lake Pepin.

Opposite: New crew member, the fabulous Kevin Arnold.

Lake Pepin or 'I Told You So'

Julie has a cousin, Kim, who is married to a truly great guy called Shad. Shad's family has fished Lake Pepin commercially for decades and as soon as I mentioned that I was contemplating the Mississippi project, he said: 'That means you will be crossing Lake Pepin, right?' I said that was the case and that the skiffs were very durable boats that could withstand whatever washes the Thames and its river craft could throw at us. Shad looked somewhat pensive and said, 'Have you *seen* Lake Pepin?' I had to confess I had not.

Everyone we spoke to who knew Pepin largely echoed Shad's concerns, and this is why. Pepin is approximately twenty miles long and the Mississippi

Below and overleaf:
A pause on Pepin and a
launch on the lake that
beckoned us with false
tranquillity.

Opposite: A wrought iron sculpture of the happily omnipresent bald eagles.

Above: The world's biggest boot – symbol of Red Wing Minnesota.

enters at one end and leaves at the bottom, making it necessary to cover the entire length of the lake. In turn, this means that a north or south wind can build up over a significant distance, transforming a modest breeze into boat-sinking waves. In addition, the lake is surrounded by the most beautiful soaring bluffs, around which bald eagles and hawks soar in search of prey. But these bluffs also exacerbate the wind, causing it to accelerate and gust suddenly, turning even placid waters into a cauldron in minutes.

As Paddy summarised: 'Here's a clue: there are several sailing clubs on Lake Pepin. Where sailing clubs prosper, rowing clubs generally don't.'

On top of the wind, you then have to add the legion of speedboats, pontoon boats and jet-skis that roam around this area. They thrash up and down the river at 50mph or more, and I knew they would surge by us to look at the boats. Imagine the army of monkeys sent by the Wicked Witch of the West in *The Wizard of Oz*. Combine the wind and the wizardry and you can see how this could be a very tricky expanse of water to negotiate – and so it proved.

The bulk of the day was a dream, particularly when compared with the battering we had received leaving the Twin Cities the day before. It was warm but not too warm, and sunny, with a tailwind to help us on our way. The scenery was spectacular, with beautiful wooded shores and tall rocky bluffs.

After twenty-nine miles of fairly serene rowing, we entered Pepin for the final five miles, having slightly depressingly pulled past Red Wing, which was to be our stop for the night.

A quick word on Red Wing. In 2008, it was ranked as the twenty-third most historic place to visit in the world by *National Geographic Traveler* magazine. Its website provides a detailed list of the many activities – from biking, hiking and rock climbing, to hunting and wine tasting – on offer. But the thing most people take away is that it is host to the world's largest boot, a Red Wing work boot, commonly worn by builders and steelworkers. Only this one is twenty feet long, sixteen feet high and seven feet wide.

Entering Pepin there was some breeze, but it was mainly a tailwind and we continued on away from the shore with light hearts for the final push. I started to notice the waves begin to build and roll, and then over in the far distance I saw some white caps. I mentioned this to Paddy in the other boat, but we felt good and pushed on. The white caps then got closer and closer until we were well and truly 'in it'. We started to head towards shore and contemplated putting life jackets on the coxes as the waves grew higher. We picked our way, exhausted, over the last few miles and reached our destination intact, but chastened. The boats had not shipped a drop, but frankly two or three more inches on the waves and we would have been swamped.

Pepin deserves its reputation for being utterly beautiful and dangerous in equal measure. Once again, the river had let us know who was boss and once again we tipped our hats and agreed.

Opposite: A view of the seemingly endless scale of the Mississippi.

Alma – the Diamond in the Rough

Most hotels we encountered down the river were peopled by the type of folk who only seem to exist in the Midwest, exuding goodwill and kinship. Very occasionally we unearthed a diamond in the rough and one such benchmark town is Alma, Wisconsin (pop. 782), the town waiting for us at our planned exit point from having navigated the last of Lake Pepin.

Alma is effectively a two-street town running parallel to the Mississippi. It was founded in 1848 by two Swiss immigrants who wanted to cut firewood as fuel for the steamboats that passed by.

The railway runs alongside the river, right through the town, and is an extremely busy line, with thirty trains travelling through each day. The frequency of these trains has given rise to the phrase, 'the Alma Pause', which is a pause in conversation. Consider this: it takes two and a half minutes for a train pulling 120 tankers to go past. Just in case the sound of

Above: Paddy, Kevin, me and our cheerleaders arriving in Alma, Wisconsin.

Above: Highly tuned athletes, carefully recovering and refuelling…

Above: Doreen and Richmond, stationed outside the wonderful Blue Door Inn, so good we came back!

these beasts rumbling through goes unnoticed, each of those thirty trains hoots its horn. Small wonder the locals sit back and bide their time.

Another striking element to Alma is the number of bald eagles. Never have I seen such a gathering – or, more correctly, a convocation – in one area. Apparently, they benefit from human intervention on the river, able to feast on the number of fish stunned or killed in the turbulent water around the dams.

The town is full of quaint shops selling river 'pearls' (found in clams in the river), and fabulously timeless stores selling antiques and curios, but it has one standout location: The Blue Door Inn. The inn is run by a truly remarkable woman, Kathy Goodman, who has refurbished this very old stone and brick building with impeccably good taste. It would not look out of place in the French Quarter in New Orleans. She embraced the project, and showered us with help, food and an endless stream of local characters from the moment we arrived in the Alma Marina to see a sign saying 'Welcome to Alma' placed there just for us.

Below: Graeme, on his throne of choice checking the road and river ahead.

Right: A long – very – goods train and the source of the Alma Pause.

Overleaf: A view of Alma from its bluff, the inevitable train passing through.

Two local restaurants opened their doors especially for us. One, Pier 4 Cafe and Smokehouse, was a true wonder, serving us exquisite ribs and pulled pork and corn on the cob of a quality only found in the Midwest. The team were agog at its sweetness and staggered to find that it had no additions – it was just picked and blanched quickly. The Blue Door Inn is a destination hotel – run there and say hi to Kathy. You will not regret it.

Man's Water

The Cambridge University Boat Club had just two boatmen over a period of a hundred years. The rowing club boatman was the very epicentre of the club. Part coach, part boat builder and repairer and part guru. The club had Cooee Phillips from 1880 to 1930, who was then succeeded by his apprentice, young Alf Twinn, from 1930 to 1980. Like hundreds of oarsmen from the CUBC, I'd heard all the legendary stories about Alf, a man who was deeply respected and feared in almost equal measure. He would always call the oarsmen 'sir', but I am sure he would have spelled it 'cur'.

One of Alf's great expressions, which he used year after year when the crews finally went to Putney for the annual Oxford and Cambridge Boat Race, was reserved for the Thames at the top of the flood tide when it was fighting against a strong headwind, causing boat-sinking waves topped with white horses. Alf would survey the scene and tell the callow young men viewing the river with huge trepidation: 'Gentlemen, this is Man's Water.'

Well, coming out of Alma, Paddy and I – two of Alf's former charges – experienced Mississippi 'Man's Water'.

The day was set to be a longer one, at thirty-four miles, and it would be just Paddy and me rowing, as we wanted to take the strain off some of our guest rowers in the days to follow. We watched the weather reports with grim faces as we saw the wind once again blowing unseasonably from the south at 17mph, gusting up to 28mph. To make matters much, much worse, we were rowing from La Crosse, Wisconsin, where the river reaches four miles wide. This in turn leads to a vicious wind against a strong tide with all the wave action you can imagine. And, as we were heading due south, a brutal headwind.

In anticipation of the conditions, we had attached our custom-made bow and stern canvasses to the skiff, but even with these trusty aids, we still shipped water. We pumped out as much as we could and continued to haul

the 450 pounds of wood with around another 100 pounds of gear (which together was about the equivalent of pulling a pig) into the headwind, mile after ludicrously slow mile. Although we did not sink, we were close. We were rowing at around 4mph but with our foot to the floor and running out of gas. At one point, we rowed up against the stern of a huge tow barge to try to get some shelter – any kind of shelter. It was pretty unpleasant being gassed by diesel fumes, but we were at least able to make some decent way into the headwind without blowing a gasket.

The jokes and stories dried up and we concentrated hard and tried desperately to support each other. It was challenging stuff, for sure.

We finished after eight and a half hours, bent and exhausted, at Lansing, Iowa. Spirits were still high as we felt we had been properly tested by this river and, although we might have bent, we had not broken. Surely the river had some respect for us too now. And we had reached another milestone: we were now finally south of Minnesota after over three weeks of rowing, having glided over the Minnesota/Iowa state line.

Two more days of rowing would see us through to Guttenberg, Iowa, where we could relax and enjoy a precious rest day. On one of those days, we spotted a large Amish family sitting on a wing dam, fishing and enjoying a picnic. They were resplendent in their typical rustic, Germanic/Dutch peasant costumes, with the men sporting Abe Lincoln-type beards. They looked at us with great interest.

As we dragged the boats ashore for a lunch break, Jeremy Dale – one of the great characters in the rowing scene and our photographer for much of the trip – went over to engage them, presumably because these were the only sentient humans for several hundred miles who had not heard his stories. It was a very happy meeting.

The Amish family, local residents on a farm, regularly visited the river for a family outing. They fished, played and ate by the river and enjoyed it in a way that nowadays so few do and so many should. They were not afraid of

Above: An Amish family, who loved our boats, fishing from the dock.

the river, and nor had tales of lost souls on the river deterred them. To them, it was a beautiful natural resource to be enjoyed to the full.

What was particularly surprising was their interest, not to say fascination, with us. It was not, as we had vaingloriously hoped, due to our winning personalities and good humour. It was, of course, the boats.

The Amish generally despise and indeed reject mechanical and garish implements of all kinds. Beyond avoiding TV and cars, for example, this attitude also extends to river craft and especially speedboats. In this area, we were fully in agreement – we hate them too and all who sail in them. So our Victorian wooden skiffs, held together with copper nails, leather, oak dowels and string, were in fact the perfect embodiment of Amish principles. The fact that these had been handcrafted and were then being propelled purely by the strength of our muscles and wills, was a source of great pleasure to the family.

I should also add that they were completely and utterly charming and, had we had just a little longer, I would have loved to take them out onto the river in our Amish-ish craft. Now that would have been one to remember.

Keithsburg

After Guttenberg and our precious rest day, we were down to a slimline crew. We were without any guest rowers for a few days and also without Graeme, our indefatigable and, until this point, omnipresent coach, who had left to go on a sailing holiday in Croatia for a fortnight. It would be odd without him, given that he was such a linchpin to the entire challenge.

I have known Graeme since I was a schoolboy, when he was my biology teacher and I was an unteachable, gobby teenager. I left school at sixteen and I was rescued from a different path by rowing, at which point I re-met Graeme. By now I knew he was a formidably fast international sculler, competing in the quad sculls at the World Championships in 1975. He just missed the 1976 Games in Montreal, but won the Wingfield Sculls – the true mark of a sculler – for many years apparently at a canter. I was in awe of his speed, but he also began to develop into an extraordinarily generous coach. He has now coached countless rowers, from beginners all the way through to international and Olympic medallists. Like the very few great coaches, he treats them all with the same patience, kindness and attention to detail.

When I first mooted the Mississippi project, he was immediately interested, especially as it was to be in his beloved skiffs. I remember him saying, 'I can't promise lots of cash for the pot, but I can give you some time.' That 'some time' turned out to be a completely selfless devotion to making the project happen. He helped train guest rowers before their arrival and was in charge of all we did on the water.

How much we might miss him was evident from his parting shot. According to the schedule, we were supposed to row from Muscatine to Wapello, and then Wapello to Burlington. However, as Graeme helpfully pointed out, Wapello isn't on the Mississippi. It's on the Iowa River.

'You sort it out,' he cheerily cried while grabbing his suitcase and

Right: Graeme imparts more technical advice. His quiet leadership was pivotal to all involved.

Above: Alex, me and Paddy after a long day. The fatigue is beginning to show in my eyes.

heading for the door. So we had the option of two alternative stopovers for Wapello, one of which was Keithsburg. 'My brother's called Keith, and he's a good egg,' said Paddy, so that was the choice made.

And what a choice. While I am certain there are hundreds of such small townships throughout the US, I very much doubt that there are many with a bigger heart than Keithsburg, Illinois (pop. 600). A Mississippi town with history, Keithsburg was once the county seat for Mercer County, and had a population at its height of some 3,000 people. Its fortunes changed when it was swamped by the huge flood of 1993 and again, brutally, in 2008. The first wiped out homes and businesses indiscriminately, in the manner of indifferent Mother Nature. The town regrouped and rebuilt, only to be wiped away again in 2008. This latter event led to many finally leaving and the only school closing. But what it did not do is kill the town's spirit.

With no hotel or motel, we stayed in a wonderfully eccentric B&B, the Lazy Acres western-themed guest house. The decor was straight out of a western, with one bed built as a covered wagon. Sian, the owner, embraced

us and brought us home-made salsa from her garden and iced tea and lemonade – heaven after a long day. That evening, we wandered into what is left of the town and went to the Eagle's Nest sports bar. It is the only bar/ restaurant in town and was started as something of a community exercise, being run by a father and his two sons who all have full-time jobs elsewhere.

We settled in, charmed by the staff, who told us the story of the town's diminished circumstances. We were truly touched by their stoicism and good humour. I took the barman aside and said that it would be my great pleasure to buy everyone in the bar a drink, just a small gesture in recognition of their kindness and fortitude and to show that we recognised their strength of spirit.

After about ten minutes, one by one or in groups they came over to us and were frankly overwhelmed by what they saw as the generosity of strangers, and international strangers at that. So taken were they, that first drinks came, then more free food and finally the owner was called into the bar and he immediately gave us all T-shirts. It developed into a truly happy, spontaneous evening where, for a couple of hours, the townsfolk of

Keithsburg were able to relive a little of the old days through stories and friendships. Once again, the magical Mississippi gave us a huge boost from the most unlikely of circumstances. Go to Keithsburg and go to the Eagle's Nest to see America at its very best.

The night-time brought massive thunderstorms, exactly as predicted. We waited until 8.30 a.m. before setting off but then, knowing we had a rest day to come, decided to go for it. We headed into the sepulchral gloom and a 12mph headwind to try to complete twenty-five miles. We decided to stick to the main channel and chance the quicker stream, but we were soon into rain. And when I say rain, I mean proper rain. They say in Ireland that it is only really raining when it is hitting you under the chin. Well, this was biblical rain. We had to pump out the boat twice, and it was so cold that poor Paddy – who was already wearing two waterproof jackets – was also wearing a life jacket for warmth, with my sheepskin over his legs and another life jacket strapping it down. And he was still shivering.

There was little respite and not one centimetre of me was dry. More alarming were the serious flashes of lightning ahead of us, with Paddy and I sharing concerned glances before counting down to the thunder that followed. Thankfully it never came too close, as I'm not sure we had a perfectly formed escape plan. We made it to Burlington after five hours of pure slog, only to find standing waves outside the marina, which was our finish. 'This could be interesting,' I said. We had no option but to chance the river crossing. We ploughed on, trying to adjust our technique to stay pushing over rather than through the waves. One, then a second, then a third started to creep over the gunnels and we began to take water in. Paddy said, 'Mate, go for it,' so I ripped as hard as I could to take us the last hundred metres and through the waves. We made it into safe harbour to find the team waiting with the kettle on in the RV and very worried looks on their faces.

Another truly remarkable day survived.

Above: It wasn't always warm! Paddy, insulated with everything we could find, still soaking and cold.

Opposite: Me with a very game Steve Webber on a very tough day.

Madder Than Us

Just occasionally, as we began to contemplate the halfway point in our quest, we were reminded of two salient and inescapable facts. Firstly, what we were attempting was in no way normal or natural and would be considered – even by extreme-sports enthusiasts – to be slightly bonkers and very possibly downright mad. This was underlined not just by the size and scale of this immense body of water, nor by the appalling conditions we ploughed through for hour upon hour, nor by the ever-present danger of capsizing or sinking or by the physical pain and discomfort. It was very often clearly underlined by the nature of the participant crew who joined us.

We had essentially raw beginners take on huge lakes. Others braved mountainous waves, wind and lately rain. And we had others who, given their ailments, should frankly have been nowhere near a boat. Take John Taylor, an old friend of mine and Paddy's, who turned up straight from seeing a specialist as he stepped off the plane in Chicago. He had a couple of small cuts on his right index finger that had become seriously infected, with the whole joint swollen and extremely painful. What did he do? He started taking horse-strength antibiotics, got strapped into his gloves, got taped up by Alex, took some ibuprofen, ignored the fact he is a golfer who has been rowing for a year or so, and rowed twenty-seven miles without complaint. At the end, his hands were bleeding through his gloves and the ends of his fingers were blistered. His backside, he said, was a personal matter between him and the long-suffering Alex. He had another twenty-nine miles to row the following day, so he said an aspirin should see him right. And we wonder how we built an empire.

Secondly, we encountered others (stand up, Ewaut!) who reminded us that we were not alone in our intensity of purpose or our slightly crackers view of what is fun and normal. And then we discovered a historic Illinois

town called Nauvoo. It is a small town with a great deal of history, much of
it surrounding the first settlement and temple of the Church of the Latter-
day Saints. They were originally run out of town and went, led by Brigham
Young, to Utah, but the connection with Nauvoo remains, as does the most
extraordinarily large and rather fetching temple, erected by the church of
LDS, in memory of Joseph Smith. All this creates a very strange, slightly
surreal atmosphere in town, which is now apparently largely Catholic (a
legacy of Étienne Cabet and the Icarians, who followed the Mormons into
town) but with a faith subjugated commercially by the wealth of the Mormon
dollar. You really should visit this town – there is no other like it. Rather like
us and Ewaut, Nauvoo has a slightly oblique view of normality, and long
may it remain.

Just when you thought it could get no more bizarre, we found a postcard
of someone who, in 1930, swam the Mississippi accompanied by his brother
in a rowboat. We know not from where he started, nor where he finished.
But how fantastic that the world has a few people who look at something
and – undimmed by the madness – say: 'Yep, I fancy a go at that.'

Perhaps not another empire, but eccentrics one and all, bless 'em.

Opposite top: The team
with the mayor of Nauvoo,
John McCarty, and the new
crewmate, John Taylor.

Opposite bottom:
The decal signage on our
trailer, which the Mayor
created and installed
overnight so we could
maintain our schedule.

Nauvoo

Aside from the eccentricities of Nauvoo, there is much to commend it, if not the truly awful hotel that we stayed in. There were some beautiful alternatives in the centre of town, and we decided to try the eponymously named 'Hotel Nauvoo' for dinner. It is sometimes said that even the blind squirrel occasionally finds a nut, or maybe it was that the Mississippi felt a degree of pity for us at the state of our hotel, but the Hotel Nauvoo is an absolute gem.

They have been in business for sixty-five years and it is a family-run affair. At the bar, I was given a beer in a glass so cold it was probably kept in liquid nitrogen. I asked to see a menu as I prised my fingers from the frozen glass, and the owner said, 'Well, here is a menu and everything is on, but you may want to look at the buffet.' The term 'look at the buffet' generally brings me out in shivers, a little like the term 'all-you-can-eat oriental buffets', but when I saw what was on offer, I realised we had hit the mother lode.

One perennial of our odyssey south had been the lack of vegetables to eat. More wings than you could shake a stick at, but sustenance of the green and fibrous variety… not so much. Imagine my untrammelled joy, then, at finding an enormous and seemingly never-ending supply of fresh broccoli, green and yellow beans, cauliflower and carrots, with a tray of catfish, three joints of turkey, ham and beef, plus chicken cooked in several fashions. All this (limitless, of course) was accompanied by a variety of potato dishes, gravies, stuffings and sauces. Lord knows, the salad buffet would have been sufficient alone! We washed the feast down with two bottles of Beaujolais Villages, and dinner for five of us, including service, was $169. We groaned out, glowing and sated. It is a truly wonderful place.

Nauvoo also left us struck again by the kindness of strangers. As we left the hotel that shall remain nameless, an unassuming guy stopped his truck to look at the boats on the trailer. Like everyone else, he was amazed at

Left: Nauvoo – first home of the Mormon church in the US.

Below: Our ever-present feathered friends.

their beauty and asked a lot of questions. One of the guys from the support team noticed his truck was advertising a sign business, and we needed some signage for the side of the boat trailer so people can connect and hopefully donate. 'Sure,' he said, 'follow me to my office.' We did so and in just under an hour he produced the most impressive set of handmade signs that looked fantastic.

'What do we owe you?' we asked. 'My pleasure,' he replied. 'Take it as my contribution to the charity.' 'How will we find you to thank you?' 'Oh, it should be easy,' he said, 'I am the mayor of Nauvoo.' So, if you ever need any signs or shirts, look up Outlaw Tees, Inc, in Nauvoo. Or just find the mayor.

Major Milestones

The next few days were a relative breeze and amazingly straightforward. We were blessed with champagne conditions of bright sunshine, gentle tailwind and a strong following stream. Notably, we passed the 1,000-mile mark. We stood in the skiff and toasted the significant achievement by sipping a dram of Talisker whiskey from Paddy's flask. He, like me, subscribes to WC Fields' aphorism: 'Always carry a flask of whiskey in case of snakebite. Also a small snake.'

Thus fortified, we eased into Quincy, Illinois, and into a marina where we found our next Mississippi gem, the Quincy Boat Club. This wonderful bunch of people were having their annual antique and classic boat show, so they thought we were part of the event! Once disabused of this notion and told we were on our way to the Gulf, they swept us up and embraced us like long-lost brothers. We were offered a berth for the night front and centre on the club pontoon. They called the local news station and I gave an interview to be broadcast in four states. We had a little damage to a metal fitting on the boat, so the captain, Ron, made one call and I was whisked off to a guy who would weld it together for us. Thirty minutes later, back with the mended item, we were having lunch as guests of the club with around a hundred members. I made a short speech at Ron's behest, and people immediately started donating to the cause. Once again, we were overwhelmed by the generosity of strangers.

As a little thank-you, Paddy and I rowed several of the elderly members around for a couple of hours. I could not have thought of a happier way to spend a day, made all the better by its complete spontaneity.

Refuelled and recharged with some real barbecue food and a glass or two of Fat Tire beer (a rare foray away from the ubiquitous Sam Adams, and one for which we felt guilty), we set off the next morning to row to Mark Twain's birthplace: Hannibal, Missouri. We were rewarded by the sight

Below: The signs for the
Great River Road, all down
the length of the river.

Left: The Mark Twain riverboat in Hannibal, Missouri, birthplace of the great author.

Bottom left: The American Queen in full flow.

Right: The bridges at Hannibal.

Bottom right: No kidding…

of our very first massive paddle steamer – all four storeys of her – and a glorious sight it was.

This section felt like several considerable milestones had been reached. We were about to go through our last lock, having been through twenty-eight since the first lock at the top end of Minneapolis. Then, not long after the 1,000-mile mark, came the halfway-to-New Orleans point. This felt hugely important and it was definite cause for another bottle of champagne. It was just as well we did, for unfortunately there was little else to celebrate that day. After our champagne stop it started to drizzle. Then it rained a little harder and then it hammered down on us, unrelenting, as we strained to keep pushing into the wind. I was wearing only a T-shirt and no shoes, as the forecast had been for warm weather.

The rain abated for a short while, before resuming over our last fifteen miles. By now, I was very weary but had no option than to keep going and get it over with as quickly as possible. Because we wanted to shorten the next day into St Louis down to thirty miles, we had arranged to go a

Above: Me and Mike Colling on a smooth day – it looked like the river had been ironed.

Above: Mike Colling, celebrating completion of his first day.

Above right: Me trying to stretch out weary limbs and back.

little further and so on we plugged. Our last straight was seven miles, but directly into the wind, which by now was building standing waves. We made towards the shore, hoping for some protection and, although we found a little, there was no stream, so progress was slow and exacerbated by lots of huge pieces of driftwood. Our two stalwart coxes had to 'slalom' along this last stretch, which in turn meant that each time they jammed on the rudder, we slowed down. It was agonising.

Once we finished, I sat slumped over my sculls as the others unloaded the boats. I congratulated our fellow rowers and then sat down on a rock, unable to move.

I knew I was close to my physical limit after so many days of ploughing into relentless headwinds, and was feeling pretty emotionally drained too. I was hugely envious of Paddy as his wife Mel was to arrive that afternoon from Australia to join us for the rest of the trip. I so wished Julie was there too as I badly needed help. All I wanted to do was curl up and sleep for a week.

This river was testing my limits, but I would never give in.

Stage Three
St Louis to Memphis

St Louis to Memphis

It was very rare for me to feel as low as I had approaching St Louis. The incessant rain, wind and build-up of fatigue had taken its toll. However, a good night's sleep and the prospect of two days' rest in St Louis was enough to pull me through the final hurdle to reach our next break.

We completed the day in bright warm sunshine, our progress only slowed by the final lock on the river. From this point on, helped by the mighty Missouri River pouring in, we would have unchecked river-flow to help us. We docked, loaded the boats on the trailer in a truly industrial wharf in St Louis, grinned for the camera, and then Paddy and I had a big old man hug, appreciating that we had passed first 1,000 miles, then halfway, and had now made it to the gateway to the South. The fatigue and concerns of the last couple of days ebbed away and the team prepared for a long-awaited evening out. We had dinner at a French brasserie called Brasserie by Niche, which proved to be an absolute delight. The quality of the bread

Above: Me and Paddy celebrating halfway, with a cheerful James Whitworth watching nervously.

Above: Entering another vast lock in St Louis.

alone made Alex weep. When the bottle of Hermitage arrived, I thought he would kiss the waiter, who I suspect would have preferred a tip.

We were taken to our hotel by an immigrant driver who I chatted with as we drove. He was highly articulate and clearly well educated. After a while, he asked why we were here and I told him about the Mississippi Million challenge. It transpired that he was from Ghana and in the US to complete his education and that of his two children. When I told him that Ghana, and especially Richmond, was the source and inspiration of this trip, he immediately began contacting the large Ghanaian diaspora throughout the States and, of course, gave us the ride for free and donated $20. Once again, we were humbled by the kindness of strangers.

The following day – a much-welcome rest day – I went to a laundromat in an area called Soulard. It reminded me architecturally of Beacon Hill in Boston, but it was much grittier, with a farmers' market and some great blues bars. The sun shone and my spirits soared. I listened to a playlist put together by Niall Murphy, a senior teacher at my son Charlie's school

(another example of the broad base of support we received), based around appropriate tracks for the Mississippi. Listening to 'Walking in Memphis', the mis-perceived load I had felt coming into St Louis began to properly evaporate. If you are ever in St Louis, go to Soulard and visit the 1860 saloon. You would need a heart of stone not to feel at home.

That evening, we visited a St Louis Cardinals game as guests of the Cardinals organisation. The scene was wonderful. There were 45,000 ticket-holders and probably a similar number at the many bars surrounding Busch stadium, enjoying the local equivalent of the craic. Everyone in our group was in great heart and I realised I was surrounded, helped, buoyed and protected by a truly wonderful group of people. Slightly embarrassed by my earlier complaining, I recognised that we were all in this together and we would triumph.

And then, just as I thought things couldn't get any better, they did. To my utter shock, amazement and delirious delight, into our bar walked Julie. She had travelled thirteen hours via JFK to St Louis and then by taxi to be

Above: A truly great evening at the St Louis Cardinals, buoyed by an unexpected and much-needed visit from Julie.

Above: The Cardinals ball park.

Opposite: Graeme, keenly interested in the ball game. Never a more apt T-shirt.

with me for two precious days before scurrying back on Sunday. For once, I was without words – certainly adequate words. It really was the perfect end to a perfect day. We enjoyed an evening of laughter, beer, hot dogs and local characters. Graeme showed his undivided interest by sleeping through a large portion of it, woken only by fireworks.

The second rest day brought brilliant sunshine and temperatures of 29°C, showing St Louis at its best. I wandered around and saw some gorgeous architecture. The buildings, in contrast to the majority outside the city, are red-brick affairs, redolent of the solidity of the commerce from which they were built. There were also Victorian covered markets, a welcome antidote to homogenous, neon supermarkets.

The city has been sadly maligned following the death of Michael Brown and subsequent conflicts in the Ferguson suburb. Admittedly, I spent very little time in the city and even less in its downtown area; however, I am a strong believer in the power of subjective assessments of new towns and particularly the folk that live within them.

Certainly, all is not positive. Racial tensions exist near if not above the surface, not helped by an overwhelmingly white police force. Relative or actual poverty exists and is evident. Many of the buildings I saw had boarded-up windows, and the sense of slightly faded grandeur was prevalent. But there is something splendid about St Louis. It has soul, spirit, chutzpah. There is a palpable energy to the city that belies the 'poor me' sense one gets in some impoverished coastal towns in the UK. There is music, there is art, there is sport and there is a community – a strong community.

I believe it is a city that is comfortable in its own skin. Its inhabitants are funny, friendly, and proud without arrogance, and I witnessed a strong multiracial mix, recent headlines notwithstanding. This city's biggest enemy is not race but a lack of commercial energy and the attendant poverty. The population has declined over the last twenty years, but a strong soul remains. As a perfect exemplar of this, we found an open-air, wander-through, entirely free jazz festival in the suburb of Old Webster. There was fabulous music and food on offer, with the legendary Freddie Webster playing sax as few can or ever could.

Were I to build a manufacturing plant or need a willing, able workforce, I would happily come here and help rebuild this rock of a town. Here is to St Louis, an unexpected gem of a city that needs our respect and our presence, not our disdain or pity. A great place.

As for the food, I have this tip: should the mood for barbecue – especially ribs – ever take you, then waste no time checking reviews elsewhere and head straight for Pappy's Smokehouse.

Throughout the US but especially in the South, barbecue is close to a religion. Heated, unsolved debates between proponents of Kansas dry rub or the wet marinades of Texas abound. However, one aspect is omnipresent and critical: barbecue is about the very cheapest cuts of meats, cooked slowly, for a very long time. Beef brisket, cooked at no more than 120°C for

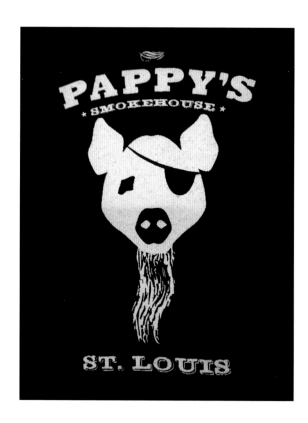

Above: Pappy's Smokehouse, arguably THE best barbecue in St Louis – a big claim.

Above: Paddy, me and the nicest man in the world (really) Dan Adams, at an outdoor jazz fest.

long hours over sweet wood, will render the collagen and connective tissue into a texture resembling soft butter. Meat lovingly prepared in such a way is a thing of great joy and beauty, and is the perfect accompaniment for slaw, corn and ice-cold Sam Adams. The food at Pappy's Smokehouse was barbecue at its finest. We ate like kings.

More Villains...

Two days on from St Louis and we encountered new villains. The wind, particularly the headwind, had long been an archvillain, a seemingly omnipresent destructive force, capable of sapping energy and enthusiasm. Now a few of his protégés had come out to play.

We set off early for our launch spot, loaded the boat with supplies, got Paddy's comfy coxing seat and various other essentials into place. Duly sorted, we set out, only to encounter a layer of thick, impenetrable fog. Trying to negotiate the hazards that the river poses on a daily basis while effectively blindfolded was not an appealing prospect. Even though we were still hundreds of miles from the Gulf, we were now regularly seeing fifteen barges being towed together, three wide and five long. They are a commanding sight, but that is the point. You need to see them.

We waited, then waited some more. In most weather conditions, whether wind, snow or rain, you can essentially take the choice to brave them. But fog? No, thanks very much. So we waited some more and eventually set off an hour and a half late to row forty-three miles. It seemed pretty clear that, although we were headed inexorably south (other than the odd detour of the river to head east, north and occasionally west) and consequently into warm and humid weather, fall was creeping up.

The second villain was the jumping Asian carp. At first, I thought talk of this huge and ridiculous jumping fish in the Mississippi was some kind of joke. Then I saw the various YouTube clips. And then I saw them myself.

At first, we weren't sure if our eyes were playing tricks on us, as we could just about make out something jumping away in the distance. As we got closer, there was no doubt. And it was clearly now no laughing matter. Bighead and Silver varieties of Asian carp can jump up to ten feet out of the water when frightened, according to the US Fish and Wildlife Service. Some

Above: A well groomed fisherman with an Asian jumping carp.

carp can also grow to sixty inches and weigh 110 pounds, and would pack a hefty punch if they hit you.

They started jumping between the oars and just missing the cox. Then they started hitting the boats. It was only the shape of the boats that kept the damn things out. They are a complete menace to all on and in the river. While they do not eat the other fish, they eat everything else, including rare snails and mussels, and food for the other river dwellers. Introduced to the US in the 1960s and 1970s, they are choking the river and causing an enormous problem. If a fisherman catches one, it is illegal to put it back alive.

A lesser spotted but equally alarming villain was of the slithering kind. As we journeyed further and further south, the river and surrounding terrain changed commensurately. Gone were the wooded glades of the North, to be replaced by wide open riverbanks, with only occasional trees and a lot

Above: Me with Simon Woods, Magenta McDougall steering, in typical conditions.

of mud. This was where we first encountered something almost universally disliked: snakes. Most snakes dislike humans even more than the other way around. Thus we only rarely see them, usually when they are sleeping or trying to absorb the heat of the morning sun to kick-start their cold-blooded systems. We saw several varieties, but always thankfully slithering away from our clumping shoes. It was their close cousins, the water snakes, that made us shudder, and one type in particular.

There was something peculiarly sinister about seeing a water snake on a river we had come to love. We were, of course, at fault for failing to maintain rigorous respect for the endless challenges the river threw at us, but we (or at least I) felt unprepared for the sight. Like the land-bound snake, most general water snakes will swim away from humans – except one. This snake goes by several different names but is `most commonly is

called the Cottonmouth, Pit Viper or, as we knew it, the Water Moccasin. These snakes are aggressive, and their bite is dangerous, occasionally fatal. Unsurprisingly, we were not keen on these particular snakes, and thankfully we only saw them a few times, all from the safety of the skiffs.

At least we had not had an encounter with that iconic creature of the South: the alligator. It is estimated that there are around 80,000 in Louisiana and Mississippi, and some of these are seriously big. In 2013, one was caught weighing 727 pounds and measuring twelve feet long. We did, however, have one main advantage – Charles Darwin. The main Mississippi, while teeming with food for the alligator, is simply too fast-flowing and so, in order to feed and survive, the sensible alligator population has learned to stick to the tributaries of the river. We often used these tributaries to enter and exit the river very, very carefully. While in the skiffs, we were entirely safe. But getting in and out of the skiffs, especially when surrounded by mud and trees, certainly heightened our senses.

Above: A 'dreich' day, as the Scots say.

Above: Me and Paddy, Marysh Chmiel steering.

Above right: A Mississippi river buoy, showing the power of the current.

Right: A permanent resident found on many of the tributaries.

... and Challenges

We had battled with big beasts, little beasts, energy-sapping winds, fog, and the vicissitudes of the dragon. But the greatest challenge now facing us lay in the maths calculations and had been placed on us by a faceless, anonymous figure working deep in the bowels of a dusty logistics office. Graeme and Paddy had been poring over the maps and had made some recalculations. The length of the river did not tally up with the distances we were rowing between stages. To be clear, they were not saying the river was longer than anticipated; what they had found out was that the maths in calculating river distances was wrong. The overall number of miles remained the same at 2,320, but they had realised that if you added the distances between stages, as per earlier calculations, the river would only be 1,886 miles long. This – most unfortunately for me and Paddy in particular, but also for the participants – would mean that some days would now have to be rather longer.

The fog day was due to be around twenty-eight miles and became forty-three. The next two days would both remain the same as scheduled, but the day before our next rest day would be fifty-one miles for me and Paddy. It was looking as though there would be one day at sixty! Paddy and I looked at the daily sheets with some trepidation as twenty-five to thirty miles had felt long enough. Add in some fog to delay starts plus our old friend the headwind, and it was clear we would need more than Sam Adams and chicken wings to sustain us! This would be the journey into Memphis – as Paddy said, it gave a whole new meaning to the term 'Memphis Blues'.

Opposite: Lunch, whilst looking carefully for wildlife.....

Gateway to the South

Perhaps not surprisingly, given its length, the journey had been more than usually well stocked with pivotal moments. We had enjoyed several to this point – starting at Itasca, the first hundred miles, reaching Minneapolis, reaching 1,000 miles, and then passing halfway. We had left St Louis and begun our journey to the lower Mississippi and the South of the US. We knew we must be getting towards the South when we asked a passing tug whether they could pick us up on their radar, as we had fitted reflectors for that purpose. The skipper replied in the very broadest southern drawl: 'Well, I can see two dots on ma screen, so that must be y'all.'

But the question was: when would we definitively be South, and another milestone reached? We canvassed opinion everywhere we could – in the locks, in the hotels, on the streets, in the shops and in the restaurants. Whenever we asked, we received a different answer.

Certain elements were always agreed. When we reached Arkansas and Kentucky, we would definitely be in the South. When we were in northern Missouri, probably for most people, that was the North. It was the bit in the middle that was more of a grey area. We had noticed a slight change in accents, but this was inconclusive. We noticed a prevalence of different foods on menus (biscuits and sausage gravy at breakfast, anyone?) and lots of barbecue restaurants, but again nothing definitive. For all sorts of perhaps obvious reasons, not the least of which was in order to define our progress, we wanted the answer.

It was with this in the back of our minds that, on a gloriously sunny day, we encountered two guys in their kayaks. Richard and Don were old friends, one from Cape Girardeau, Missouri, the other from across the river in Thebes, Illinois. I would guess they were in their late sixties and liked to spend time pottering up and down the Mississippi. They were genuinely

surprised and happy to see us and loved the boat we were in. They were sad that so few local folk used the river for pleasure as they were all too scared of its fearsome reputation. However, for us, this was the perfect time to tap into local knowledge as to whether we were yet in the South.

The answer from our Illinois contestant was 'South of St Louis' – the accents change and those living in southern Illinois think of themselves as being from the South.

From Cape Girardeau came a different response: 'You head five miles south of Cape Girardeau and you come to a steep hill down to the plain. It is flat from there to New Orleans. The accents are different, and they grow cotton down there. That's where the South starts.'

Still no definitive answer, then, although as we rowed out of Cape Girardeau past the hill, the land did flatten out. Suffice to say that our next stop would be Kentucky and by then we would, unequivocally, be South.

Above: Richard and Don, welcome companions and two of the few recreational paddlers on a treacherous river.

Right: Our $10 radar reflector…

A Cultural Revival

Personally, I think that cultural and regional identity are laudable traits, notwithstanding decades in which segregation and discrimination ruled. In a country with an extraordinary homogenisation of cities – Starbucks everywhere, identical shops and malls – cultural identity has been eroded continually and I believe it is an important element, the absence of which is striking.

If you travel to Liverpool in the UK, then catch a train for thirty minutes to Manchester, the first thing you will notice is that the accents are remarkably different. Between these cities is Wigan, which has an accent entirely different to either of its larger neighbours. This is very much the case throughout the UK, from the West Country drawl of Devon and Cornwall to the impenetrable dialect of Newcastle and Durham. How, then, can a country as huge as the US, built on mass immigration, have such little variation of accent? Of course, the slow southern drawl is identifiably different to Brahmin Bostonian, but generally, accents are remarkably similar.

Then there is the food. If we strip out the universally interchangeable stores and restaurants in shopping malls, where identical Cinnabons can be eaten in DC or California, most supermarkets have identical foodstuffs. I have been in many huge supermarkets and seen, for example, cheese cabinets the size of minor aircraft hangars. In these, one can buy seemingly endless variations of American cheeses – most called Monterey Jack, all of them untroubled by flavour or character of any kind. Add to this the 'deli meat counter' and you find the same: endless variations of the same water-, sodium- and nitrate-injected hams that are absent of any identifiable texture and flavour.

In this melting pot of humanity and land of plenty, how can this possibly be? Well, here is one man's theory.

Opposite: The glorious daily sunsets. This view never got old.

Overleaf: Graeme, Paddy and me, slipping along smoothly and quickly.

Above: A big stretch, Cambridge flag resplendent.

I have noticed a very common trait when discussing family histories with folk. The common theme is that the first generation, often with zero or little English, forbade their children to speak their own native tongue and forced them to learn English. They wanted their children to be American, with all the hope that that term entailed and which had brought them from their own homelands. They did *not* want the children to be Swedish-American or German-American or Italian-American, they wanted them to be American. Thus the headlong pursuit of a single language began, and with it the steady erosion of any regional or – God forbid – internationally influenced variations. It was the beginning of the flat, Midwest accent that has become the go-to desired received pronunciation of newsreaders across the US.

In the same way, these immigrants wanted to fit in with their new neighbours. So nationally cherished dishes became tame, watered-down and bastardised versions of the original. Steak haché from France became the hamburger when adopted by the tens of thousands of Germans. Strong, exquisitely flavoured cheeses had their strength removed and all became 'Cheddar'. Fabulous veal and chicken sausages from Germany became red-skinned monstrosities filled with unmentionable offcuts and labelled 'frankfurters'. Food and accent, both emasculated by a common desire to blend in, became pale and homogenised to the point of being unrecognisably different wherever you are. But there is change afoot...

Over the last twenty-something years, there has been a growing trend in both these areas. People are now taking positive steps to rediscover not only their roots, but all the heritage that goes with those roots. They want to announce, advertise and celebrate their history, and thus an interesting reverse of the original position has occurred. Now, it is entirely common to ask from where someone came, to want to know whether someone is African-American, German-American, and so on. What was once shunned is now embraced. Indeed, it would now be strange to simply say 'American' without some prefix.

This new-found enthusiasm for heritage has spawned something else: a rediscovery not only of the foods of their ancestors, but crucially a rediscovery of the flavours of these foods. The US, with its astonishing agricultural capacity, will soon be making the world's best Parma and Serrano hams, the best kielbasa, the best Gorgonzola or Camembert. Finally, the fastest and strongest trend of recent years has been the rise of microbreweries. And wherever you see an interest and support in a local microbrewery, I guarantee you will also see an interest in regional foods. Even the supermarkets are taking note, trying to replicate the feel of local farmers' markets in the presentation of some food products. This change is taking root and, in time, I believe we will see a rejection of the commonplace and dreadful packaged nonsense masquerading as food, and we will see a healthier and happier population.

Who knows, we may even hear a regional accent or two. And then perhaps we will also be able to put the North–South debate to bed.

Left: The curiously shaped lake trees in Arkansas.

Bottom left: A typically difficult exit after a long day. As we travelled further South, these daily extractions became extremely challenging.

Right: Carrying a very heavy skiff up a rocky path.

Bottom right: Paddy and me, boats safely stowed.

State of Mind – and Body

With twenty-two days left before we were due to hit New Orleans and the end, I had been reflecting on my feelings. A couple of factors had started to weigh in.

The first was psychological. When I was trying to prepare for this marathon, I spent hours on the rowing ergometer. While the erg, as it is unaffectionately known, is a very effective physiological training tool, it is painful and also pretty boring. On the long sessions, I used to get an image in my head of a hamster on a wheel. The longest single sessions I did were an hour and a half long. It was very hard work, with your legs going dead as the edge of the seat restricted the flow of blood to them, and in any event

Above: Magenta, Paddy and I set off on a balmy day.

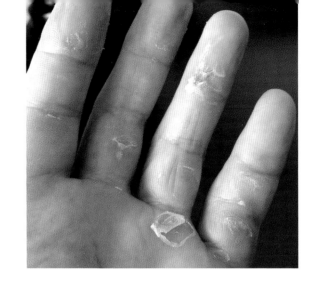

Top right: Wear and tear on my hands.

Left: Inevitable patched repairs.

it was uncomfortable. The toughest part of the ninety-minute pulls was the fifteen minutes just after the hour mark. By this stage, you had completed the lion's share of the work and the end was in sight, but it was still a little way off. Mentally, that last quarter of an hour was always truly gruelling.

At this point of the challenge, I felt like I was in that fifteen-minute slot after the hour mark. I had now rowed around 1,500 miles, with about 800 to go. I could almost see the end, but not quite. The six days into Memphis and the next extended rest point were really draining psychologically. Physically I was strong, but I was mentally weary. A continual stream of participant crew members undoubtedly helped, but I was longing to reach Memphis, from where I would definitely be able to see the end.

The second factor was that I was suffering pretty badly with mosquito bites. We were staying in a magnificent setting next to a lake in Tennessee, but unfortunately that meant still water, which with hot humid days was a perfect combo for these purveyors of misery. My powers of attraction to a mosquito are, as yet, unparalleled. I have shared rooms with guys on rowing trips where they end up sleeping like dead men, and I emerge looking like a pizza. It has never been the risk of malaria that bothers me, rather the fact that the merest nibble engorges subcutaneously to look like someone has slipped a quail's egg under my skin. Sure enough, I was eaten alive on the first two days and was able to count twenty-two bites on my left big toe and twenty-seven bites on my right big toe alone! Sadly, the rest of my feet, ankles and legs up to my knees were also covered in bites, and I was slightly concerned that some of the bites on my feet were looking infected. The number of bites was truly tedious but, as I told myself, it was only pain – a mere flesh wound.

Fortunately, help was at hand from a good friend we had made in Hannibal, Missouri: Dave Davies, the world's happiest undertaker. He had brought us a couple of presents to help us on our way, with this accompanying letter:

To John Pritchard and our new friends on the
Mississippi Million,

*I know a friend who has a neighbour who has a cousin
somewhere between Hannibal and St Louis who sometimes
makes stuff for his friends. I, being a friend, and you all being
my friends, am providing you with some refreshment from
the hills of Missouri. The bigger mason jar is called Apple Pie
and is probably 80–100 proof. Serving size: one shot glass.
The smaller is called Missouri Moonshine. It is 180–190 proof.
Yes, it is the real deal. Use sparingly. A little dab will do you.
Straight or mixed. It may not be for everyone. It does have
multiple uses: paintbrush cleaner, solvent for cleaning axle
bearings, a great steriliser, killing grass in concrete cracks, etc.*

Some rules apply:
  - *Do not break the glass*
  - *Keep away from fire and flames*
  - *Do not take it through airports or customs*
  - *Do not put in an empty stomach*
  - *Wait until all work is done. Sit and sip and don't ever gulp*
  - *Most important – never operate machinery after or during
    consumption.*

*Have a safe and memory-filled trip. And remember what Sam
Clemens said: 'A naked man rapidly loses all credibility.'*

*Your fans,
Ma and Paw from Hannibal*

Above: The marvellously
clear instructions on the
bottle of moonshine.

Opposite: An indication
of the scale of overnight
rain. We received 5 inches
and the river rose 7 feet...

Yet More Miles

Coming into St Louis, we had had five inches of rain overnight. Apart from filling the top boat on the trailer, necessitating endless pumping out before we could move, the rain had a truly seismic impact on the river. Over the following twenty-four hours, it rose seven feet. Unbelievable, but true. That increased the flow a great deal, but at that point we were still in the lock-and-dam system, so we did not really benefit. The second impact was to scoop up all the wooden detritus left on the riverbanks. These were not bits of driftwood you might spot on the Thames and other rivers, but ranged from smallish pieces through to whole trees. These boat-wrecking behemoths became deeply sodden and sat just at or below the surface, making them devilishly difficult to spot. If you did have the misfortune to hit them, there would only ever be one winner.

The river steadily fell back to pre-rain levels but, with more storms forecast, it seemed a surfboard would be more useful than a skiff for reaching New Orleans.

Above: The Mississippi keeps rollin' on…

Above: A skiff's eye view of barge traffic.

Above right: Me with Sarkis Zeronian on a very tough day of (yet more) headwind.

Overleaf: A 42-barge load and an ever-present threat. Someone nervously asked, 'Don't you in a skiff have right of way?'

Then there were the mileage miscalculations by the event planners, which had turned into truly egregious clangers. We knew now that the total river miles of 2,320 did not correspond to the total miles of the combined sections as listed. With twenty days left, I was counting them down, as you might imagine. I had been particularly happy to see that there were two very short days of nine and seventeen miles. Graeme looked hard at each day and found that in fact the seventeen-mile day was seventy. It was not hard to imagine our reaction to that piece of joyous news. And there were several other revised distances – all of which were, naturally, longer.

One of them proved to be the day that took us into Memphis. Now that we were into the last month, guest rowers were arriving every other day as momentum built. I was with the amazingly stoical Sarkis Zeronian, definitely a man to have alongside you in a trench. He is a huge man who, if he had hinges, would unquestionably be a door. We had known that it was due to be a long day, but the recalculations now meant we were facing forty-nine miles, the first eighteen of which would be into a beast of a headwind

Left: Simon Woods, me and Magenta, arriving on a sandbar for lunch.

Below: The ever-willing Alex Conty, helping us exit.

around 12–15mph, gusting to 25mph. Sarkis barely blinked and worked steadily, with me following him, and Paddy steering. These was amongst the heaviest winds we had seen, and he bore up remarkably well as we pushed through water churned by tugs pushing thirty-five barges, more than twice the size of the biggest we had seen in the North. After this pull, we swapped in Paddy for Sarkis and the two of us paddled steadily over the next thirty miles, dropping Sarkis back in for the victory paddle over the last mile into Memphis. It was a great achievement, but boy was I tired.

Left: A typical view of a headwind day.

Bottom left: Simon Hotchin stretches his 6'6" frame.

Right: Matt Brittin celebrates the start of his first day. I know what to expect…

Bottom right: Magenta, me and Matt. Alison, Paddy and Marysh.

Legends of Memphis

Friday night in Memphis. It almost says it all. Here we were in one of the iconic cities of the US and possibly of the world. Revived by champagne, we set off down Beale Street, which has to be one of the very best music venues. We gorged on dry-rub ribs and cold beers before walking into BB King's club, which had a band playing and the whole venue dancing. It was fantastic. Although slightly sleazy in daylight, the street comes to life at sunset and parties until the small hours every night, with the weekend the highlights. Just wandering down the street, you hear fabulous blues from just about every bar and we would have been happy in any of them – and were, in fact, happy in several!

Hungover and happy the next day, we eased through the morning, doing laundry and minor repairs to the boats (thankfully, just wear and tear), then all set off for the tour of Graceland. Volumes have been written about the

Below left: Trouble comes in fours… Julie, Mel, Gillian and Magenta before a night on Beale Street.

Below and opposite: The scene in every bar in Memphis, one of the truly great cities.

shrine that was Elvis Aaron Presley's home, but we all thoroughly enjoyed it. Updated and guided by personal iPads, we wandered through the 1970s kitsch decoration, all against the backdrop of an Elvis soundtrack. Frankly, we were all staggered at the scale of his achievements and legacy. Who knew he had been in thirty-one films, all of which were financially successful, let alone the estimated one billion records sold and still selling? Amazing.

Day two of our stay was more sober in every way. We visited the National Civil Rights Museum and were prepared for a litany of man's inhumanity to his fellow man, from the beginning of resistance during slavery, up to and including events in my lifetime.

I am not sure who had the extraordinary idea to create a civil rights museum at the back of a nondescript, down-at-heel motel, but it was a stroke of genius. The Lorraine Motel, where Martin Luther King was assassinated on 4 April 1968, has been largely preserved and the room where Dr King stayed is intact, down to the contents of the ashtrays. The room marks the end of the journey through the museum. The main displays are shocking, as they should

Above: The Memphis Civil Rights Museum. A deeply moving and vitally important exhibition of man's inhumanity to man.

Above and above right:
The preserved facade of the Lorraine Motel forms a permanent part of the Civil Rights Museum. It is the site of the assassination of Dr Martin Luther King.

be, and deeply relevant to today. Possibly, for someone of my age, one of the most alarming facts is that I was ten when the assassination occurred.

Early in our odyssey, way up in the North in Minnesota, I shared a car ride with a guy who gave me a lift back to our campsite from a restaurant. He was a white, college-educated professional we had chatted to in a bar. He asked me about race and the UK and I explained that racism, along with sexism, remained a cultural issue, but that I hoped that the younger generation was in a different, better place to ease towards greater equality. He said something to me that stuck with me throughout our journey and will unquestionably stay with me. I found his comment clear, precise and deeply depressing. He said, 'Every country, even the most civilised, has its own racial scars. But in the US it is a scab – it is just below the surface and it is not healed.'

It would be entirely wrong to say that we encountered racism continually – we most certainly did not. But we found it an ever-present and deeply unwelcome companion, especially so as we ventured further south.

There were many incidents of casual racism. An elderly white woman in Louisiana remarked to me in a store when she heard me talking to someone about the Confederate flag: 'You know, that Mr Lincoln did not give us [the southern rebel states] one dollar in compensation when he took away our workers [i.e. slaves].' She said this with no trace of irony.

Another white man, this time in Mississippi, referred to the Civil War as 'the recent unpleasantness', and he did so with a rather wistful sense of regret, I thought. We rarely saw a Confederate flag flying on anything that might be considered an official building, but we saw many on private homes and especially on bumper stickers of cars belonging to the euphemistic 'good ole boys' (and girls, I guess).

The most shocking example was in New Orleans, two days after we finished. I was travelling back from a computer store in a taxi driven by a white driver. He was a New Orleans native and probably in his early seventies. He asked me if I had eaten at Mother's cafe, near my hotel. I told him I was a regular and he extolled its virtues. He also added that the original owners, two brothers, had an unusual approach to local support. He said: 'Back in those days, if a cop killed a nigger, he took a little heat, so the brothers looked after him – made sure he had a ham from the kitchen.' I did not think he meant a black cop.

Ultimately, the reason I found it all so depressing is not, per my Minnesotan friend's comment, that racism exists. It is that there seems to be a presumption in many areas that it does not exist or is diminished. Racism, in my experience, is still very much a scab.

By current estimates, the membership of the KKK in the US is around 5,000 (according to Cal State University).

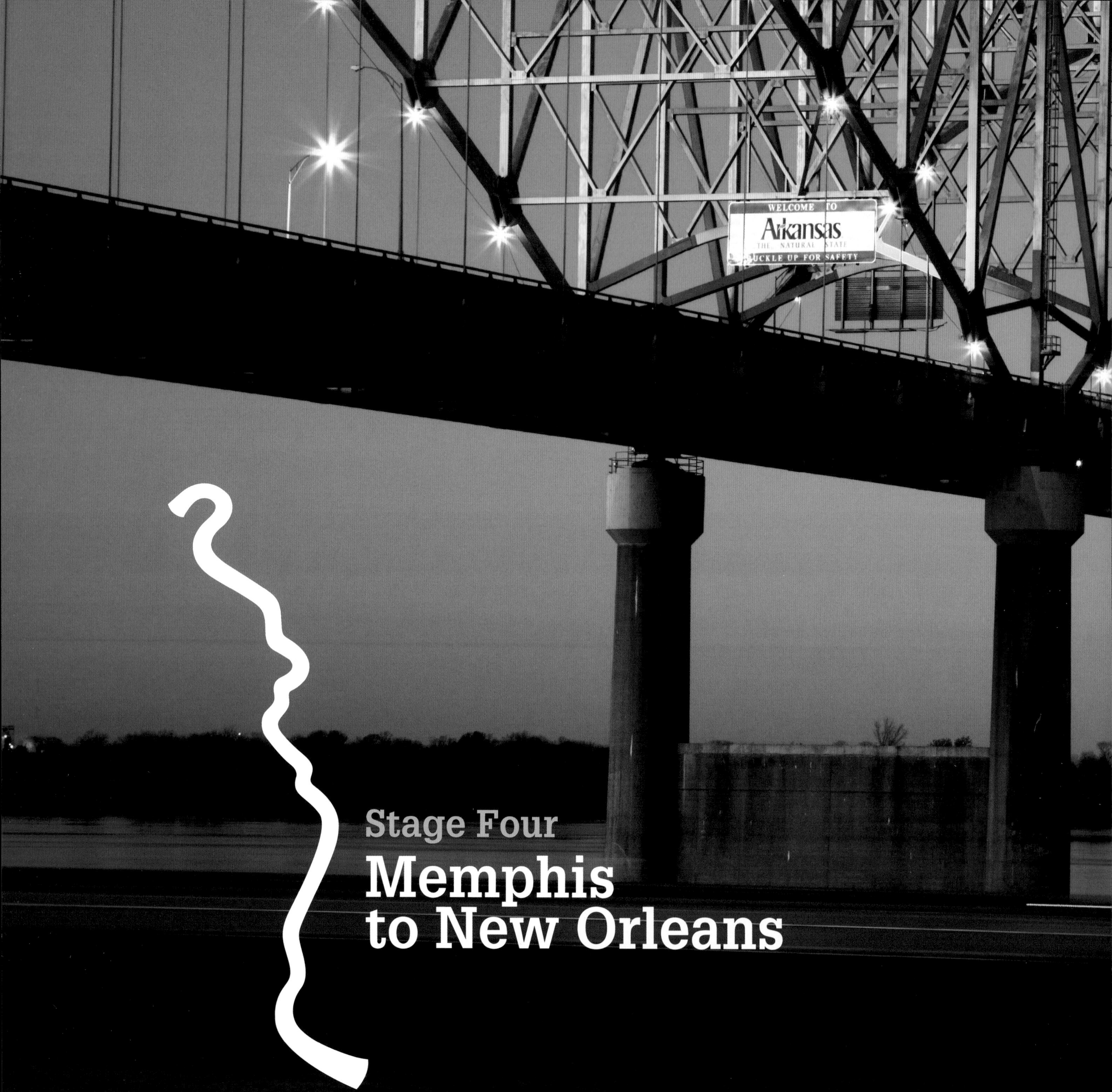

WELCOME TO
Arkansas
THE NATURAL STATE
BUCKLE UP FOR SAFETY

Stage Four
Memphis
to New Orleans

Right: Safe overnight harbour for the stars of the show.

More Miles on the Clock

Here's an insight to the last section of the journey: the 'recalculations' that were required had played havoc with our plans, and in particular with our plan to wind down before a ceremonial arrival at New Orleans. The last section was to have been eight, then six, then four days to the finish with two rest days afterwards. Now it would have to be seven, then a 'rest' day in which Paddy and I rowed twenty miles, then eleven days straight. In addition, the daily miles had increased to make up the miscalculations to high thirty- and forty-mile days. The most obvious issue, therefore, was that this was now going to be especially gruelling through to New Orleans. It would be tough, not least for Paddy and me, but for all the participants joining us who now faced increased loads but still willingly accepted them.

Early in our journey, although we were not truly cognisant of it at the time, we had been incredibly lucky with the weather and the river. There had certainly been bad days – indeed some truly testing days – but we had also had a lot of fine weather for at least the first six weeks, especially when crossing some of the big lakes. However, the river dragon had stirred and decided that a) the removal of rest days was no big deal, and b) the significant increase in daily miles right through to the end was something we could take on the chin. In its omniscience, it decided we needed something to truly test us.

The first suggestion of a change in the weather came when we were all woken by our mobile phones with a message: 'Tornado alert. Take shelter.' Of course, we did nothing. But it did herald a shift and an unwelcome one. The prevailing wind in the southern US in October is north-easterly. We had not only a south wind, but it was strong – very strong – gusting continually. And, to cap it all, it was fixed in position for at least the next ten days.

To put that in perspective, our row out of Memphis was thirty-nine miles. The following day was thirty-seven miles (thanks to our revised calculations).

Left: The skiffs look like they have glided like birds onto a sandbank. How we loved these boats.

This equated to approximately fifteen hours of pulling into a relentless wind, which battered us to the extent that we had to literally push the oars forward into the wind. We had the further joy of endless tugs, now pushing packs of up to forty-two barges. The power and energy required to push these monsters created swells on an industrial scale that ran the length of a football pitch. They threatened to swamp the boats, and we had to pump them out at most rest stops. They also created whirlpools that flung the boats one way or another or tried to spin them round. Small wonder that there are virtually no pleasure craft on the river. Most locals regard the river, with its swathes of commercial traffic, as something extremely dangerous to be avoided at all costs.

Two days of these conditions and we climbed from the boat hunched and aching, then tried to stretch out taut backs and hamstrings. It was not in any way fun, and this was the prognosis for as long as the forecast showed.

What made a huge difference was the friends who just kept coming, smiling, rowing like there was no tomorrow, buying drinks and dinner and generally propping us up. After thirty-nine miles into a beast of a wind, I was on my knees. They, however, said they loved it. Nuts.

I had also received a private letter of support from my son Charlie, which gave me a much-needed lift. Charlie's contribution could not be overstated. At the start of the trip, he had willingly given up five weeks of his long-awaited and precious summer holiday to make himself available for any work that was going. He steered the boats and rowed whenever called upon, which was especially brave as he had a partially torn tendon in his right wrist. He put up and packed away tents, cleared campsites and packed up vehicles. He made tea and brought drinks. He helped Alex when required and sold T-shirts for the cause – the English accent helped in this regard, I think. Most importantly of all, he did all this unbidden and without a trace of complaint. I was truly, hugely proud of this fifteen-year-old boy who surely wanted to hang out with his mates and meet girls but instead helped a charity raise a ton of money for children in desperate need.

Left: A Louisiana riverboat.

Bottom left: An unexpected joy – a hot air balloon display over the river traffic.

Opposite: Simon Holden, one of the catalysts for the project, smiling at the beginning of the day.

Overleaf: The river, astonishingly, seemed not only endless but also just to get bigger.

Clarksdale

After yet another battering day on the river into a headwind, we arrived at a nondescript exit ramp, thick with Mississippi River mud (the eponymous pie is a perfect replica in all but flavour) to find an excited Alex. He was unusually ebullient as we hauled the boat from the water and loaded it onto the trailer. 'You wait till you see this town,' he cried, and we thought he had taken leave of his senses after nearly three months on the road. But how right he was.

Unless you are a dyed-in-the-wool blues fan, there is probably no reason to have heard of Clarksdale. There are so many places in this area – Memphis and Nashville, to name two – that scream jazz, blues, rock and roll, bluegrass and country, and drag fans from all over the world. But Clarksdale is the birthplace of the blues, a mecca for aficionados. It was here, as legend has it, that the young Robert Johnson went to the crossroads at midnight

Above: A modern convenience store.

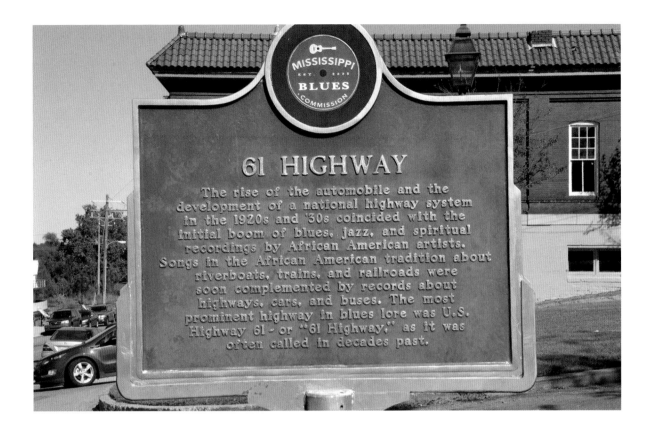

Above: 61 Highway – the intersection of commercial traffic and art forms.

and sold his soul to the devil in exchange for the blues and unbelievable guitar skills. Clarksdale is an antebellum treasure, built on the backs of slaves and King Cotton, where, in the early to mid-1840s, the town had more millionaires per capita than New York or Boston. Those days having long since passed, the town is in its second incarnation.

Clarksdale today is an absolute gem of a place, with wonderful cafes and some outstanding little hotels. We devoured lunch in a lovely cafe and then walked upstairs to find our accommodation: converted apartments in an old warehouse, the quality of which would shame Manhattan. Then there are the blues bars.

The first night of our stay found us in Red's Lounge. It is as authentic a blues dive bar as exists. In a deep southern drawl, the locals described it to us as: 'A dive, but you gotta go there.' The building (a term I use loosely) looks as if it was condemned between the two World Wars. At around 6 p.m., a large black cast-iron trolley appears outside, and the charcoal

Left and right: Ground Zero – the epicentre and birthplace of the blues.

is lit for the barbecue. At around 7 p.m. (timing is rarely precise in the South), very large men carry very large cooler boxes into the gloom of the bar. Sometime around 9 p.m., the absurdly well-fed figure of Red turns up, the flickering lights turn on, the musicians – mainly acoustic, occasionally electric – arrive and the session begins. This is precisely the type of place that McKinley Morganfield – or, as he is better known, Muddy Waters – played the blues. One of the main acts that night was Cadillac John, a ninety-year-old harmonica player and singer. Bored halfway through a couple of numbers, he said to his band, 'That's enuff o' that,' and the band then obligingly moved on to the next track without missing a beat. The entertainment was worth every cent.

An alternative and slightly more upmarket option is to visit Ground Zero, owned by Morgan Freeman and located on Blues Alley. Go there, eat fried green tomatoes with gitback sauce, drink ice-cold beer and listen to the best delta blues on the planet. We were royally entertained by 'Razorblade', who had introduced himself to Graeme in a local cafe, saying:

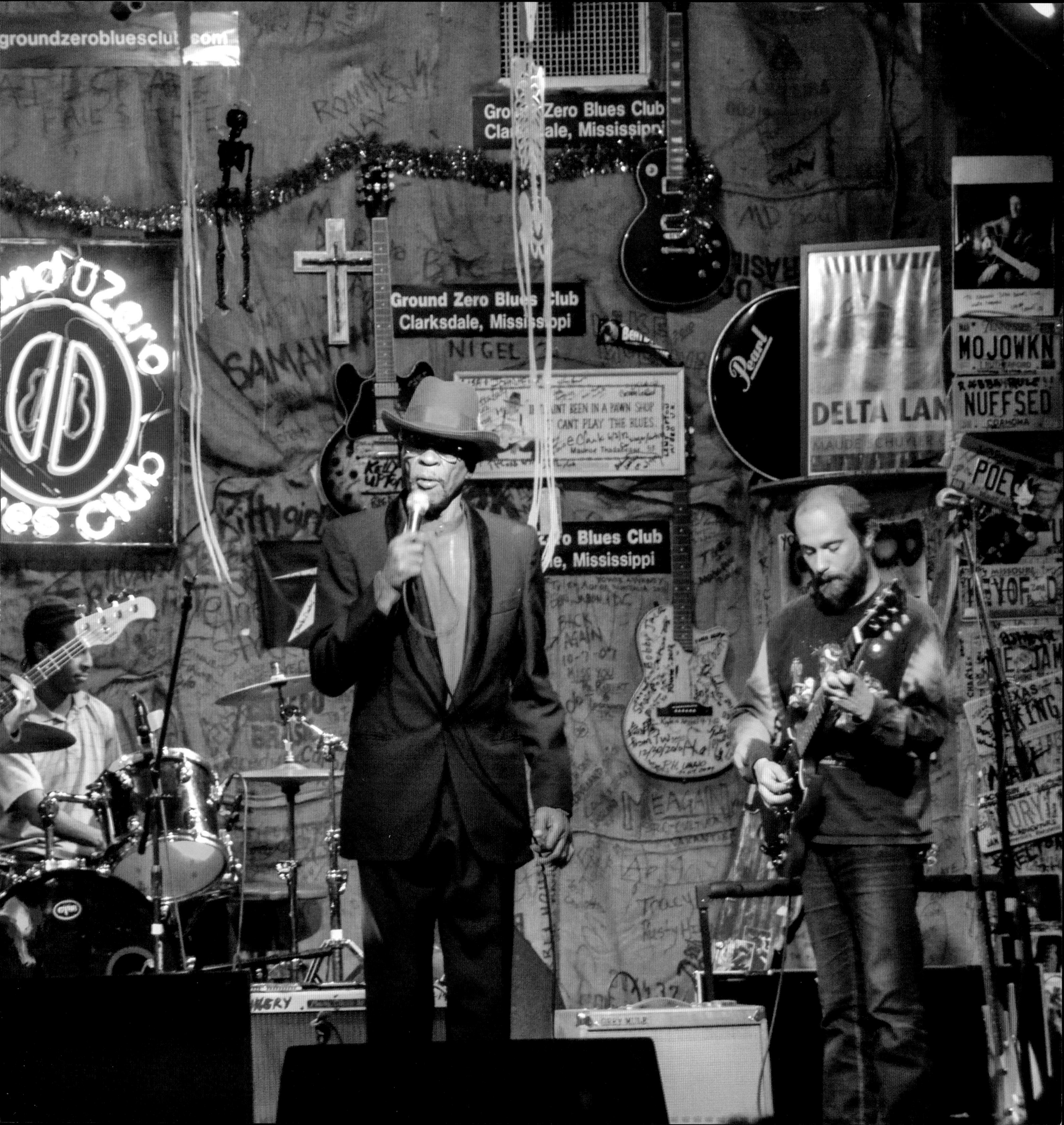

groundzerobluesclub.com
Ground Zero Blues Club
Clarksdale, Mississippi
Ground Zero Blues Club
Clarksdale, Mississippi
Zero Blues Club
Mississippi
Pearl
DELTA LAN
MOJOWKN
NUFFSED

'Hi, I'm Razorblade, something of a blues legend around here.' All credit to him – he is.

There is even, with world-class eccentricity, a dedicated blues museum run by a Dutchman. Whatever else this book encourages or discourages, do consider visiting Clarksdale and relaxing there. It is a haven and I will most definitely be going back.

The quality of the accommodation, hospitality and food was all excellent. Just as well, because the trying days continued. Leaving Clarksdale we faced, on current form, almost an easy day: twenty-eight miles with only a gentle headwind. The next day was fifty miles, with more south wind blowing and what seemed to be a convention for barges. At one point, we had three of these monsters passing each other at the same time, two going one way and a third going the other. This still left room for the two modest but beautiful skiffs, but the turbulence was enormous.

Given the heat (32°C) and 90 per cent humidity, we were thirsty in a way that is difficult to describe. We rowed for seven and a half hours, stopping for a few minutes every half-hour. After a while in this heat, we were glugging at our water bottles, filling our stomachs, but almost immediately upon resuming rowing, finding ourselves thirsty again. When we finished, there was not a spare drop in either boat.

King Cotton

While we may have debated the positioning of the North–South divide at length, there could be absolutely no doubt about what territory we had now hit. This was Cotton County.

Travelling down the east bank of the river, through Missouri, you see rolling hills and yet more miles of corn and soy. You then descend onto a plain, flat landscape that stretches on and on with hardly a tree to break the view. You notice that instead of tall rows of corn stalks bulging with fat cobs, or fields of short, stubby bushes with pods of beans (the ones that, steamed, cost £5 a bowl in London restaurants – how the locals laugh at that!), you suddenly see straggly, knee-height bushes that appear to be decorated for Christmas. Then you get a little closer and you see mile upon mile of these extraordinary balls of cotton. I could not resist getting out to feel these funny little plants and, sure enough, they feel exactly like cotton balls, except protected by sharp hulls underneath, which spike and cut your fingers if you are not very careful. This is still the dominant crop here and has been since 1800.

The population in 1800 in Mississippi was 8,850, of which 3,349 were slaves. The amount of cotton exported was zero. By 1860, the population

Above: A sharecropper's shack in Clarksdale.

Above: King Cotton – for a London boy, a source of endless fascination.

was 791,305, of which 436,631 were slaves. Cotton exported: 535,100,000 pounds. The wealth created – very much the underpinning rationale behind maintaining slavery – was astounding. The price of cotton went from 5c to $2 regardless of the increase in production. But before you condemn the South alone in this hideous picture, remember that the bankers of New York lent money and provided insurance for the industry, while the shippers in Boston and New England did very, very well. And the vast majority of the crop was bought by the mills of Yorkshire and Lancashire. Fortunes were made. There were more millionaires per capita in Greenville, Mississippi than in New York City. But no longer. Mississippi is now the poorest state in the union, although its character shines through – and guess what? Cotton is still king.

On top of the additional miles, the weather had deteriorated and was making a tough situation that little bit tougher. We had been seeing tornado warnings for a little while. We started to take them seriously once we realised the impact of this on our already-crowded schedule. By now we had only one rest day remaining in the run-in to the finish. That ended up being spent hunkering down in Greenville. The rest day was full of storms and rain, but thankfully the tornado missed Greenville. Sadly it hit further upstate, but at least we and the boats were safe.

Gin Palace, Southern-style

The unscheduled stopover in Greenville meant that we were a day late to avail ourselves of the hospitality of Paddy's uncle, Jim Phillips, a long-term Louisiana resident, social catalyst and generally fabulous guy. As soon as Jim knew about Paddy's involvement in the project, he embraced it and us fully. Jim is an agronomist and consequently knows every farm and farmer in the state, as far as I can see. First off, he managed to find us accommodation at a gem of a hunting lodge owned by James Oscar Thornton, the scion of a long-established Louisiana family. The whole family rallied around and supplied a fabulous supper, followed by a return fixture with pancakes, bacon and coffee at 7 a.m. It was a joyous stop and we were all very sad that the rearrangement of our schedule meant we had not been able to stay there a couple of nights. But, as James Oscar said, 'you took too long to get here.'

Partly as a result of Jim's network of mates in the area and partly due to folk we met, we had gathered a significant collection of characters. Hank, from Greenville way, was sufficiently larger than life that we were reasonably sure light actually emanated from him. He introduced us to Boll Weevil, a true river rat, who had a large riverboat and offered to follow us, plus any guests, all the way by river from Baton Rouge to New Orleans. It was starting to feel like it could be quite a party on the last day. Then there was Billy.

After our next day's rowing, Billy (arguably, producer of the most cotton in Louisiana – and that is a *lot* of cotton) took us to see his cotton gin. The word 'gin' is the common diminutive applied to the Longford 'cotton engine' as developed in the late eighteenth century. Its emergence and full automation created the wealth of the South and ensured the importance of slavery for decades. It is fair to say that the very idea of a cotton gin is enshrined in written American folklore along with Mark Twain, riverboat steamers and southern cooking. When the suggestion was made of an invitation to visit

Opposite: A 'gin' palace: A 'modern' version of a cotton engine factory.

the gin, everyone on the team immediately asked to accompany us. Nothing any of us had seen before prepared us for what we witnessed.

Although nowadays the gins are housed in gigantic barns or factories and turn out tons of packed, cleaned cotton, the actual process has not changed since Eli Whitney invented it in 1793. As Billy commented, 'Those guys were brilliant, the same basic pattern is still in use today 200 years later.' At their peak, the gins ran twenty-four hours a day, seven days a week during the cotton harvest. Now, with increased competition from India and China and therefore less cotton planted, the machines run for twelve hours a day.

It was an astonishing sight. Truckloads of 'unclean' cotton – full of seeds and therefore useless for material and clothing – were dumped at one end, dried, processed through the gin, and then the clean cotton was baled. This smooth process all happened within a few very noisy minutes. The age-old way the economic system works is that the farmer gets the cleaned 'ginned' cotton and the person who owns the gin gets the seed (which is sold for cattle feed and next season's crop).

This wonderful experience took a truly unexpected turn at the sumptuous dinner that night at Billy's glorious antebellum house by Lake Bruin. We were served frogs' legs, fried oysters, Louisiana shrimp, seafood gumbo, etouffee, red beans and rice, and smoked tenderloin. It was a feast and we fell upon it. The company was equally entrancing. We were in a house filled by characters, the least interesting of whom were us!

Fascinated by what we had seen at the gin that day, I was keen to quiz Billy further about the operation. There were about 120 workers at the gin – mostly men but some women, all African-American – and I suggested to Billy that, as Mississippi is the poorest state in the union and unemployment is so high, he must be a local hero. He looked slightly puzzled before revealing that all the workers were from the local penitentiary. Shocked, I probed further: 'So, rather than using a local workforce, you have labour for free?'

'No, I pay the prison, and I think the prisoners get 50 per cent.'

'What do you pay the prison?'

'What I want,' came the reply. As for the locals, he assured me that they were content on benefits and were disinterested in working.

Now, I don't know what conditions were like in the local state penitentiary and I am sure it is preferable to spend your day at a gin than inside a cell, but I couldn't help wondering if I had drifted inadvertently onto the set of *Cool Hand Luke*. What was clear to me was that the farmers and gin owners did well out of this arrangement. The locals? Less clear. It certainly struck me as a lazy assumption and a slur on the local community that they would be happy to live off deeply unattractive US state benefits rather than earn their own money. I doubt it's ever been put to the test or will be anytime soon.

Leaving Lake Bruin, and a mere forty-four-mile row later (although in decent conditions so we had no grumbles), we were down to just nine days. I had been wisely counselled by Julie to savour every moment as they would be truly precious. Indeed they would be, and I intended to.

Of all the Luck...

We had been joined by Marysh and Alison Chmiel, both hard-as-nails rowers and very welcome additions. Marysh is also a maker of truly exquisite furniture out of the Alexander Workshop, and had made for me and the project ninety presentation boxes from the same mahogany as the boats. Inside these small, perfect little boxes were individual oars, carved by hand by Marysh and Al's children. These little gifts, presented when participants finished their stint, brought tears to the eyes of recipients and were one of the highlights of the trip.

A throng of Louisiana locals joined us to wave us off and wish us well in fabulous sunshine. We paddled a few strokes away from the bank and, as Marysh was adjusting his foot stretcher, I noticed we had some water in the boat. I asked if Al had a sponge as the stream pulled us further from the bank. As she was looking for one, I noticed that we were taking in water, and at some rate. We were, in fact, sinking, and sinking fast. I whipped the

Above: Alison and Marysh Chmiel.

Opposite: Marysh explaining boat construction.

skiff round as quickly as I could, whistled to Graeme and the shore crew and frantically got us to shore.

Above: A potential disaster.

Above: The magician, Marysh, at work.

The other boat came in and we lifted out the Richmond and put it on trestles. We lifted the footboards and, sure enough, just by the centre of the boat was a major hole, with the mahogany splintered up inside the boat. It was obvious that as we had come ashore yesterday we had hit a sharp rock at the wrong angle and caused the damage. Thank goodness we were within shouting distance of the shore – a smaller leak and we would have gone down later, miles from the support crew. It was unbelievable luck that it happened when it did, especially when we considered the beating the boats had withstood upriver through rapids and rocks. But we also had one other staggering piece of luck: we had Marysh.

He immediately gathered up some tools and went to work, aided by Paddy. He painstakingly removed each splinter of wood individually and laid them on pieces of kitchen towel to dry in the exact order of removal. He then set about the same procedure on the underside of the boat. Then

Above: The result of the magician's work almost undetectable on the outside of the skiff.

he cleaned up as only he could and dried out the mess around the hole. He waited for it all to dry out before putting it back together, glueing each fragment with epoxy. It was mesmerising to watch – no brain surgeon would have taken more care. He then scraped, millimetre by millimetre, until the repair was barely visible. It was like watching a world-class magician in slow motion. He covered the two sides in tape, to allow the epoxy to fix while we went on the water. It took four hours to complete, and the craftsmanship was such that if you had varnished over his repair you would barely notice it. Remarkable.

We went afloat at midday and paddled into yet more southerly headwind for thirty-five miles. We plodded along resolutely. The heat of the day and the waiting for the repair had left us all a little jaded, but today had been another adventure for the team, for sure. It was astonishing and humbling to me, the way in which the team continued to receive setbacks and simply dealt with them, quietly, efficiently, and stoically.

Body Creak

The countdown was by now in full swing. I had checked and rechecked the calendar and, whichever way I viewed it, we had only six days until we reached New Orleans and the end of our journey of 2,320 miles down this most majestic of rivers. But we did still have six days to negotiate. A strange series of sensations and emotions were beginning to well up as I approached those last sections now that we were clearly in sight of the line. But we were also on the edge in other ways too.

Both Paddy and I were aware of the warnings of the physiologists, nutritionists and medics, who had cautioned us that towards the end of the journey we were going to struggle. They were unconcerned about our ability to row between four and nine hours every day for three months. They knew that we were driven to succeed. What concerned them was the accumulation of fatigue and how that might impact us over the last few weeks. We were by no means dismissive, but we were frankly sceptical, especially as we seemed to bounce back even after the most gruelling of days (of which there had been no shortage). Then, with six days to go, Paddy and I realised that many of their predictions were now beginning to come true. We were both now carrying residual problems.

Paddy had a sore back that was seemingly getting stiffer each morning. Alex was manipulating him, and he was trying to loosen up each day, helped by ibuprofen. He also had some nasty blisters under the callouses he had built up during the first two months. These were hardcore nasties and even he now had to wear a glove. He also confessed to feeling weary, which I could echo only too easily. It was a measure of our level of fatigue that we stopped in the boat and quietly shook hands as we passed the 2,000-mile mark.

I had cuts on my hand and foot that had taken five weeks to heal. I had some sores now on my backside that were not blisters or chafing from the

Opposite: Nearly three months of daily effort starting to catch up.

seat, but residual sores from sitting and rocking back and forth twenty times a minute for several hours a day. I was also deeply tired. The fact of the matter was that we were just not healing, as each of these ailments would, in 'normal' life, disappear in a day or two. But not now.

On the other hand, we now had – whisper it – a very light northerly wind! In addition, the weather front parked off the Louisiana coast, helped by a similar front somewhere around Memphis, suggested that the weather was fixed until at least the following weekend. This, as you can imagine, was a source of unalloyed joy for us after literally months spent crunching into a southerly headwind. We also had some absolutely stellar crew members with us, and Julie and my son Charlie would be joining us in the run-in to the end, along with a few other very good old friends. There was a true sense of momentum building, and I was doing my very best to maximise this last week. It was hard to keep a lid on our excitement, conscious that this river would unquestionably continue to test us, as it had for three months. But I was also trying to enjoy every minute of the rowing, the scenery, the atmosphere and the wonderful Louisiana folk. We were definitely teetering on the edge of something truly special. But we were not there yet.

Diet – A Few Words

Prior to beginning our Mississippi challenge, Paddy and I were advised that our bodies would be consuming epic quantities of calories and would thus require equally epic refuelling on a constant basis. While this conjured up guilt-free images of endless pizza, bacon sandwiches and pasta, the truth of the matter was somewhat different. The trip had two wholly unexpected effects on our diet.

Firstly, the first two weeks had been incredibly draining physically and we were almost continually hungry to the point of ravenous but, beyond those two weeks, our desire to eat subtly changed. We are both experienced rowers and have years of technique on which to rely. However, the nature of what we were doing was very different to anything else we had done in that we were paddling, slowly, steadily for several hours a day. Instead of trying to go as quickly as possible from A to B, now we simply had to endure and suffer for hour upon hour. As a physical challenge, it was much

Above: The vehicles – unsung heroes of our trip.

Opposite: Gavin Sayers, me and Mel, power along.

closer to an Arctic walk than a rowing race. As a result, our bodies reacted in much the same way as the Arctic explorers' – we became more and more efficient. Along with this efficiency came a decreased need for calories, and our overall intake reduced dramatically.

What was of greater importance was that we ate regularly and at key times. Breakfast became utterly critical. Twice I missed breakfast and twice I 'hit the wall' a few hours later. Once you are in deficit, you never really catch up. After breakfast, eating something – whether it was a bite of banana, some nuts or raisins – at every thirty-minute rest made all the difference. Miss just one, and fatigue crept in.

Secondly, our desire for certain foods increased exponentially during the weeks of toil, while at the same time we could not stand the sight of other foods. Our bodies were telling us the right things to eat, and it was this aspect that took us most by surprise.

The two food groups that we quickly discarded were not ones we would have guessed at the outset – carbohydrates and refined sugars. Doughnuts,

Above: The Louisiana
Salad – note the greens.

biscuits, neat sugar, burger buns, pizza and the like became anathema. Like vampires confronted by garlic, we recoiled. However, we craved protein and green vegetables. We genuflected at the altar of broccoli. We worshipped a big juicy steak. Spinach, courgettes, cabbage were our targets. Chicken, fish and lamb were searched for on every menu.

This regime had become, sadly, harder and harder as we ventured further south, the southern approach to green vegetables being somewhat outré. While they have some remarkable and wonderful vegetable dishes (such as fried green tomatoes), these would inevitably be served with fabulous white crabmeat topping and usually hollandaise sauce. In the end, we decided to count deep-fried pickles (yes, slices of pickle, dipped in batter and deep fried) as vegetables. That was how desperate we were. While the physical demands of the trip were inevitably going to strain our creaking bodies, the paucity of green vegetables that *looked like* green vegetables at this stage was not helping. On the upside, chicken wings and Sam Adams would always help lift the spirits, if not the oars.

Cancer Alley

Another day, another milestone. Four days out from New Orleans marked the last day that Paddy and I would row together on this trip. It was also a little emotional for the two of us, bound as we now were by literally thousands of miles together down this river. I could not even begin to try to encapsulate what a hero he had been on this trip – but we were both conscious of ending our partnership in a boat together. A small matter for others, but rather bigger for us. Suffice to say, tears were shed. For the last four days, we would have guest rowers with us, so while we would be on the water together, we wouldn't be in the same boat. We joked that after literally hundreds of thousands of strokes together, it was a shame we couldn't get into a race sometime soon! We did, however, have a crack at the top-speed record for the trip: we ripped hard for twenty strokes and hit 14.3mph. Not bad for two old geezers and a Victorian skiff!

Above: The petro-chemical section.

Below: Barges, Barges, everywhere.

Overleaf: Our boats felt even more vulnerable – Paddling with Jeremy Dale.

So to Cancer Alley, a rather unprepossessing title. We had been warned constantly that the river from Baton Rouge to New Orleans is a beast of a very different colour, with full-sized ocean tankers and barges over a quarter of a mile long. People had also warned us of the chemical plants all the way to New Orleans, giving rise (allegedly) to the largest concentration of cancers in the local population, hence the name they give to this section of the river. However, they assured us that four days out there would be fine.

Baton Rouge was named by the earliest French explorers who, on venturing up the river, came to a point marked by a large cedar log, covered in blood and the carcasses of animals. This pole marked the territory boundary between two native tribes and, given its prominence and gruesome colour, it was unsurprisingly called Red Stick. And so the name stuck.

Although the setting by St Francisville was nicely rural, once on our way we were quickly aware of a very pungent smell wafting at us on the wind. It was a nasty combination of something chemical that caused your throat to catch as you breathed, enhanced by what smelled a little like organic death of some kind. It reminded me of the story of the always-blunt Duke of Edinburgh arriving in Lagos in the 1960s with his equally outspoken equerry, Lord Rupert Nevill. When the plane door opened, the Duke stepped out and said, 'My God, Nevill. What is that ghastly smell?'

'I believe it is shit, sir,' replied Nevill.

'I know that,' said the Duke, 'but what have they done to it?'

The smell set the tone for this section, which was unusually serpentine

Above: Paddy and Derek
Mayne pass a tanker.

Overleaf: The ships just
got bigger and scarier.

– a trait we would now have all the way to the Gulf. As we came towards the first of two bridges at Baton Rouge, I glanced over my left shoulder and had a look around the bend in the river. All I could see on both banks were endless chemical and power plants, belching white smoke into the blue sky. It may, of course, have been steam, but the sites from which it came looked pretty foreboding. We plodded on, through several tugs with huge barge loads, to the site of Baton Rouge proper, marked by two huge stationary riverboats, now used as floating casinos. These are, in common with all the others we had seen, operated by members of various Native American tribes, I suspect as some sort of appeasement after decades of disadvantage. Somehow, it seemed to me appropriate that the original Red Stick, with its gruesome cargo, had been replaced by a glitzy, ersatz riverboat – a modern-day totem if ever I saw one.

This stretch of the river posed significant difficulties in terms of trying to find suitable exits, as the land either side is owned now by petrochemical businesses and as such is a potential target for terrorists. Therefore they –

Homeland Security and the coastguard, who are responsible for security –
are less than keen to have strangers pitching up at their plants. After a very
hard, seven-hour row of forty-two miles, we finally came ashore on a sandy
bank next to some industrial-looking pipes. We were very pleased to see
our support team arriving with the trailer. The oil-company security team,
who sprang up at the same time, were perhaps less pleased. In fact, they
were incredibly helpful and gave us a hand to load the boats. They even

Above: We enter the
outskirts of New Orleans.

Above: Paddy and Derek passing an old New Orleans cotton mill.

Overleaf: Modern New Orleans.

told us where a good spot might be to launch the next day. Quite clearly, that same sandy bank was not an option.

Three days to go and we found ourselves with a ludicrously easy paddle of around twenty miles. Compared to the forty-two miles of the day before, it was barely worth changing into rowing kit! We weaved between moving supertankers, avoided massive barges, and swerved around solo tugs and launches. The general (not universal) attitude of the skippers of the big tows

that work the river was disappointing. We listened to them talking to each other on our VHF marine radios and the comments between them about us had been at best dismissive and at worst derive and insulting. It was OK that they referred to us as 'kayakers' and only once in three months did anyone call us 'rowers', but I balked at them saying, 'These guys don't know what they are doing or where they are going.' Frankly, given that between me, Paddy and Graeme, we have about a hundred years' experience of navigating on rivers and we had so far not run into bridges, dams, locks or run aground – all of which we had seen them do – it came to a head when one of them said to us: 'Why don't you just jump off a bridge if you want to kill yourself? Out here you will get run over by ships.' Ah, southern hospitality at its very best.

By this stage, endless plans were being hatched for various bars and restaurants, and what we wanted to drink when we finished. (Sam Adams? Champagne?) I could not begin to imagine at this point how it would feel, but I was truly beginning to feel excited, emotional and not a little relieved. I had had significant doubt about whether I had 'the right stuff' to accomplish this challenge. At this moment, the indication was that I just might.

Opposite: A grain tower, ready to unload.

Overleaf: The Natchez riverboat, a New Orleans Icon, which played 'Row, row, row your boat'as we passed.

St Crispin's Day

'That he which hath no stomach to this fight,
Let him depart; his passport shall be made
And crowns for convoy put into his purse:
We would not die in that man's company
That fears his fellowship to die with us.
This day is called the feast of Crispian...
He that shall live this day, and see old age,
Will yearly on the vigil feast his neighbours,
And say "To-morrow is Saint Crispian:"
Then will he strip his sleeve and show his scars,
And say, "These wounds I had on Crispian's day."...
We few, we happy few, we band of brothers;
For he to-day that sheds his blood with me
Shall be my brother.
Henry V, William Shakespeare

Could there be a more appropriate quote for this journey, the team and its achievements? Lord knows, blood had been shed by those toiling at the oars, lifting boats and equipment and keeping us on schedule.

The last day of our odyssey down the Mississippi was St Crispin's Day. The Crispin's Day speech from *Henry V* is one of my all-time favourites and I could think of no more auspicious end to our journey than that it should fall on 25 October and give me an excuse (not that I really needed one) to quote a line or two.'

I wrote these lines in the blog I had been writing throughout the journey but, in truth, it was something of a distraction, as the prospect of finishing the

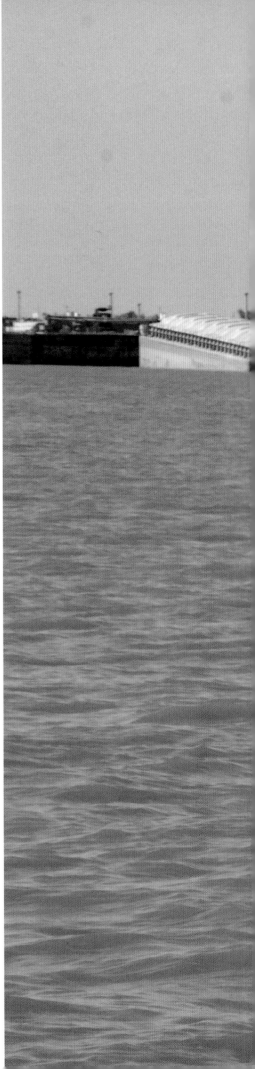

Above: The supporters watch the final extraction.

Right: Paddling to the finish line.

Overleaf: The finish line – a sharp turn off our Great River.

following day was pretty overwhelming. How could I in any way adequately summarise my feelings at this point? I could not.

Over the course of the penultimate day, our group had been swelled by serried ranks of family and friends. There were twenty-odd people on the bank when we finished our thirty-six-mile stint and there would have been many more if they had been able to find us!

For the last day, our Louisianan friend Boll Weevil had managed to secure a launch, generally accustomed to depositing workers on tankers,

Above: Paddy in all his formidable, hirsute glory.

Centre top: The final extraction.

Centre bottom: The final stroke of the project

Right, top and bottom:
High spirits and a sense
of celebration on the
supporters boat.

now masquerading as a party boat, to take everyone with us on the last thirty-six miles of our journey. I very much hoped to make this a celebratory paddle, with people dropping into the boats so they could feel that they had been part of the last day. The sense of expectation was rising and folk had been plotting and planning, with clinking bags of champagne and beer (in the end no one could make a decision about what to drink).

But just as I should have been beside myself with excitement, I felt as flat as a pancake and all I could think of was my band of brothers. This was

exactly the feeling you get when you have striven for a specific target – an Olympics, a World Championship, a Boat Race – and then you achieve your objective. Somehow, oddly, you always feel flat for a while. The enormity of all this would take weeks to sink in, I suspected, and perhaps I would only really begin to see it through the prism of others' vision, as mine was too narrow. This was a moment of quiet reflection. But waking up on the final day, to bright sunshine, I was sure I would be ready to embrace the whole scene and to savour some of what we had done.

Above: Finally, many hands to load our boats.

Right: Julie hugs me – much needed and very emotional.

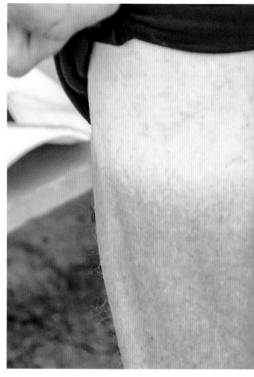

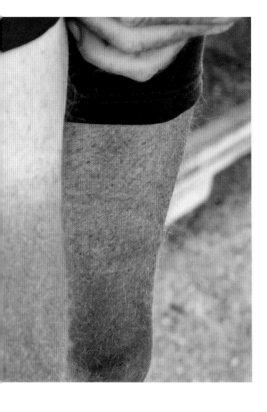

Top left and middle:
Paddy explaining it was
easy. Paddy's leg suntan.

Bottom left: Julie, me
and Charlie.

Bottom middle: A
relieved me and Paddy.

Left: A big man hug
in progress.

New Orleans

New Orleans, Louisiana, 26 October 2014

After 2,320-odd miles of toil, pain, laughter, wonderment, hospitality, friendship, kindness, headwinds, rain, thunder, lightning, tornados, blood, sores and Sam Adams beer, we arrived in New Orleans at 2.35 p.m.

Happy St Crispin's Day!

Top row left: Me, Carin and Paddy.

Top row middle: Vital refuelling in process.

Top row right: Paddy, Keith Broughton and Sean Kennedy plus trouble 1, trouble 2 and trouble 3…

Bottom row left: Dan Adams, Jerry Rees and Chris Mahoney.

Bottom row middle: Paddy with his angel wings.

Above: Alex, Jerry and Helen.

Above: Water from Itasca, water from New Orleans…

Top row: Derek
Mayne and me, suitably
refreshed.

A beardless Paddy.

A pensive Magenta.

A beaming Julie.

The team, searching for
another bar

A happy, but thirsty and
slightly dangerous group.

Bottom row: The great
Patrick Walsh and me.

Typical New Orleans
apartment.

Carin Zaleski.

Epilogue

Opposite: Carin, Fred,
Billy and Dan.

Epilogue

Everyone tells you to expect a certain sense of deflation on return from these extended projects or expeditions. But very few people have actually been on this kind of extended project and so most in fact have very little understanding of the sense of emptiness when the routine and, most importantly, the purpose has been removed from your life – abruptly and with little ceremony. So I found myself back in London, utterly delighted to see Julie, but with a house full of builders, cold, windy weather, and feeling a remarkably poignant degree of what I can only describe as 'flatness'.

There had, of course, been some ceremony on completion. The celebration party when we finally hit New Orleans, after nearly three months on the water, had been as big as could be expected. Our arrival at the dock had been extremely emotional. It was only within the last two miles of our epic journey that the prospect of actually achieving our goal finally hit me. I had managed to row a huge distance, fuelled by unwavering support, grim and focused determination, and adrenaline. It was, I think, partly due to fatigue and partly to the loss of the adrenaline on completion that great waves of emotion began to surface.

Finding an exit point from the Mississippi in New Orleans is so much more complex due to the height of the levees constructed after Hurricane Katrina (sadly for many poor folk, this was very much a stable door closing after the departure of the horse). Our intrepid support team found an 'out' downstream of New Orleans, but reaching it presented two problems. Firstly, it was a very tight left turn off the river, made more challenging by the flow rate. Secondly, only one boat could pass through the neck of the entrance to a small dock, from which the boats would be winched out of the river.

Paddy, ever the pinnacle of good sense, spotted this and asked the eminently sensible question: 'Pritch, do you want to go in first or shall I?'

It was at this precise point that the combination of fatigue and emotion kicked in. I replied, without consideration of practicality: 'Pad, we either go in together or not at all. We have covered 2,320 miles together and we must finish together.' Paddy attempted reason – a faculty that had temporarily escaped me – and calmly told me it was not possible, but I was having none of it. I insisted that the two skiffs be side by side with the oars pulled across to make one wide craft.

The crew members appeased me (possibly because I was by this stage a swivel-eyed loon), and duly we lashed the boats and, with great effort, eased carefully into the dock. I am certain that not one soul among the huge crowd waiting to greet us knew or cared a jot which boat came in first. But it mattered hugely, deeply and emotionally to me that Paddy and I came in side by side.

The celebrations started at midday at the Galvez restaurant in the French Quarter, jazz band in the background, drinks in hand. The copious food matched the mood of unbound happiness. I made a truly pathetic attempt to thank everyone, but the enormity of what I was trying to convey overwhelmed me. At this point, Simon Holden, who was on the board of Right To Play at the time and took over from me as chairman, stepped into the breach. It was Simon who had been one of the first to tell me that I could and would do this thing, and who had provided incalculable support from inception to the very end, when he rowed into New Orleans with me. Not only did he provide critical emotional support, but he also played a key role in securing finances to fund the project, meaning that 100 per cent of the money subsequently donated went to the charity. His speech – generous, kind, funny, poignant and deeply moving for all attending – delivered all I wanted to say and so much more. It was one of the lifetime memories I will cherish.

At this point, some three hours into the party, I said that I desperately needed a quick thirty-minute nap to recharge my batteries for an evening out. It was then that a large bottle of Glenmorangie was secured and I found myself with Paddy and others, polishing off the whisky, the need and desire for a nap disappearing.

We were magically transported to the candlelit Lafitte's Blacksmith Shop bar. I was drinking Hurricanes (a New Orleans cocktail of rum, fruit juice and grenadine), interspersed with pints of beer as a balance. I was wearing Mardi Gras beads, while Paddy was wearing a pair of multi-coloured angel wings. The drinks escalated to the extremely potent Long Island Iced Teas and the idea of food was sensibly mooted. A group of more sensible people (admittedly, a low bar at that point) went ahead and managed to convince a restaurant to take us. I am embarrassed to say that apparently I ate a steak with my hands, and we were gently asked to move on when we started dancing on the bar, the tables proving insufficiently robust. I'm not sure what happened to most of the others, but to my mind I saw out the night in some style.

The following morning I had a truly catastrophic hangover. No one need know the more organic side effects, but suffice to say that I could not drink fizzy water on the basis that it was too noisy, and it took me eight minutes to put on my underpants.

Once back in the UK, I spent ten days essentially secluded at home, with almost zero interest in engaging with anyone other than close friends. I avoided responding to emails or answering telephone calls and texts, and generally hunkered down. I was, essentially, hibernating. It was viscerally clear to me that I needed to be alone.

One calm, bright, autumnal day, I found myself over at the Skiff Club. I took out a very old single skiff and some equally venerable oars and set off. It being midweek, there were no other crafts on the water and a blessed lack of commercial traffic. I saw a Thames tug with a single barge, and the sight made me laugh so hard I had to stop rowing. The paddle up to Hampton Court was beautiful, peaceful and astonishingly short by comparison to the daily long haul of the Mississippi. I found the trip hugely comforting (other than my backside, which definitely grumbled) and the distance ludicrously easy. Before the project, a ten-mile round trip to Hampton Court had seemed a long outing. Now it felt like a warm-up.

I ate my fill and more of broccoli, cabbage, spinach and anything else green. I ate endless amounts of clementines, apples and kiwi fruit. I drank green tea. My body was extremely grateful, but mentally my ability to process the scale of the Mississippi project and what we had achieved still eluded me. As the days and weeks became months, the project and what it meant began to crystallise and it became obvious that there were two distinct categories – subjective and objective.

The project had begun with my madness and the idea to row the Great River on my own. This developed over more than two years of planning into the shore team, the London support team, supporters in pretty much all corners of the world and, of course, the fifty or so equally mad folk who undertook part of the journey. We were all, in our own way, content that we had delivered on our individual responsibilities and delighted that we had completed our task. However, there was one aspect that deeply affected all involved and that was entirely unexpected: the project had created its own magic.

Those most affected were unquestionably the participants. Without exception, all who came to the river became emotionally connected and were truly reluctant to leave. Many returned, simply to be part of this alchemic positivity which had no central wizard but rather was created by the sum of the good will of all involved. It also infected those further afield, and to this day I meet people transfixed by the journey and the story. Most humbling has been those who say, without a trace of doubt, that their involvement was a highlight of their lives. Had I even suspected that this might occur, I am certain I would have been too daunted to get beyond

confessing to Julie that I wanted to have a crack at the Mississippi. What this so clearly underlined was that everyone who was involved, directly or indirectly, contributed to what we achieved. I am convinced that without the contribution of even the most modest supporter, we would have failed. The achievement was absolutely collective.

As for the 'core' group of participants and supporters, they have flattered me beyond words by asking if I have any plans for anything else similar. They have made it clear that if any such plans exist – of whatever kind – they are in. One has suggested skiffing, slowly and with great care to stop at any and all decent restaurants, on the Canal du Midi down to the Med. Paddy and I have discussed rowing the Murray River in Australia, with me becoming Sancho Panza to his Don Quixote, but there is the inescapable issue that for quite large stretches there is no Murray River! I quite fancy paddling the Danube with Julie. Thus far, these are still being explored over many beers but with no resolution. I am happy and proud that our band of brothers, our fellowship of the river, remains strong and committed to something else.

While it was a hugely draining experience for me in particular, there is a reason why so many people who run marathons often run another, even though the pain of the event is intense. In the immediate aftermath, I was broken and physically and emotionally exhausted. I could not have contemplated another project. But time is a great healer, and the pain is soon replaced by that nagging thought that perhaps next time you could do it that little bit better, or faster, or for longer, whatever your target is. So although no current plans exist, 'never' is a word I abhor.

Then there is the objective outcome of our trip. Again, let me start with New Orleans. When I stood in the Lafitte's Blacksmith Shop bar, giddy with grog and fatigue, into the bar walked one of my great friends. An old crewmate in two Olympics, he was injured and unable to row with me, but as a true buddy he turned up for the party. It was wonderful to see him. Over our second drink, he asked me where we had reached on the fundraising. I told him I was not sure but at that point I thought we were close to $780,000. He nodded and put his arm around my shoulder and said, 'I'll top it up to a million.'

It is difficult to describe the emotion at that point – clearly relief and also a huge weight lifted. With the value of hindsight, I now realise that my initial target of $1,000,000 was massively hubristic. I now know just how hard folk work to raise $1,000 running marathons in the desert or wherever. If I had known then what I know now, the target would have been much more modest.

In fact, the final total (a slightly difficult-to-define number as funds came into different Right To Play offices at very different times) was around $1,270,000. This was an astonishing number to everyone, especially me. We then discovered that an arrangement had been made with the Canadian Overseas Development office to match raise unrestricted funding for a given period and that the Mississippi project fell within this ambit. Thus the final figure was around $2,500,000.

And what have these funds achieved? Because the funds were unrestricted (meaning that they could be used when and where most needed at any given moment), they were deployed largely in sixteen countries across Africa, Asia and the Middle East. The funds helped hundreds of thousands of children with education, conflict resolution, health, gender and disability awareness. The impact this has on the lives and expectations of these multitudinous children is difficult to overstate. But, in addition, the children take these lessons to their families and communities and the tangible impacts continue to grow.

The money is primarily used to train the volunteers, who are almost all teachers within the schools and refugee camps. They are taught the broad variety of games developed by the RTP educational professors in Toronto.

These games are specifically devised to encourage learning around issues such as HIV/Aids, malaria, conflict resolution, and gender awareness, and specifically adapted according to region, gender and cultural sensitivities. Importantly, none of these leaders are paid in any way – they take the courses because they see first-hand the impact they have on the communities. School attendance rates rocket, and disease-related issues diminish as the children teach their parents about hygiene, mosquito nets, and the like.

At the beginning of the project, if you had told me we might be able to help sixteen children, it would have been worth it. Together, we helped sixteen countries.

And finally, what of Richmond Chirrapah, the inspiration of our story? First and foremost, he is well and living with his family who know something of his impact and are proud of him. In fact, he is living with his aunt in a town called Ashaiman, quite close to the school where we first met him. He is enrolled in the Gebathar Prep School and, according to the latest update, is now learning to read and write, and of course still captivating everyone with his smile. He is still in contact with the RTP coaches in Battor, Ghana, but his disability means it is impossible for him to understand what he has achieved. God knows, it is hard enough for me. We also spent several thousand dollars of the funds we raised to build a spectacular playground at the Three Kings Special School, dedicated to Richmond. The playground is specifically designed with the disabilities of the children at the school in mind and they love it.

As for me, I think of Richmond daily and the impact he had on my life and the lives of countless others. The Mississippi Million project seems surreal from this distance, even though I am frequently asked about it. However, from time to time, it occurs to me that we did manage something that has made the world just a little bit kinder and brighter for those who need it most. And for that, I shall be indebted to everyone involved for the rest of my life.

Participants

Stage One

Stage Two

Stage Four

Stage Three

1 Mark Wilson 2 Harry Williamson, Grace Williamson & Charlie Pritchard 3 Matt & Lucy Horgan 4 Sarah & Rachel Vickers 5 Mark Vickers & Charlie Pritchard 6 JP, PB & Stephen Peel 7 JP, Gavin Sayers, Mark Vickers & PB 8 Michael & Jane Pasternak 9 Jeff Hughes 10 Kelly Ennis 11 JP & Johann Koss 12 Pamela Schroeder 13 Harry Williamson 14 Freddie Gate 15 JP & Chris Gate 16 Charlie Schroeder 17 Kevin Arnold 18 Trish & Dan Adams 19 Julie Williamson, JP & Harry Williamson 20 PB, Stuart & Margie Chase, & JP 21 Steve Webber & JP 22 John Taylor & JP 23 Peter Gate 24 Mike Colling 25 Alex Conty & Stephen Gillespie 26 Maeve Gillespie 27 Jerry Rees & JP 28 James Whitworth 29 Julie Williamson 30 Chris Gate 31 Mel Broughton, PB, Michael Pasternak, JP & Simon Irish 32 Richard Stow & JP 33 PB & Tom Barry 34 Gillian Mulcahy 35 Sarkis Zeronian & JP 36 JP & Mark Wilson 37 PB, Simon Woods, Fran Docker, Will Docker, Andy Trahar & JP 38 Charlie Green & JP 39 Simon Hotchin & JP 40 Jim Eyre, David Ellis & Alex Conty 41 Repton Salisbury & JP 42 JP & Matt Brittin 43 Mark Machin 44 Marysh & Alison Chmiel 45 Jim Pew 46 Jim Pew & Jeremy Dale 47 Gavin Sayers 48 Simon Holden & Derek Mayne 49 JP & Julia Dale 50 Catherine Silva & Magenta McDougall 51 Kyra Felisky

Index

Page references in *italics* indicate images.

Adams, Dan *135*, *236*, *242*,
    251
Alexander Workshop 196
alligators 16, 140, *141*
'Alma Pause, the' 98, 100
Alma, Wisconsin 98–100, *98–9*, *100–1*,
    102–3, 104
American Queen, The (riverboat) *124*
Amish 106–7, *107*
Arkansas 144, *154*
Army Corps of Engineers (ACE) 31, 35, 46,
    56, 68
Arnold, Kevin *89*, *98*, *250*
Asian carp 16, 137–8, *138*

bald eagles 34–5, 40, *94*, *95*, 99, *121*
Baton Rouge, Louisiana 192, 209, 212, 213
Billy (cotton producer) 192, 194–5, *242*
Blue Door Inn, Alma *99*, 99, 100
blues music 131, 142, 168, *168–9*, 184–6,
    186–7, 188, *189*
Brasserie by Niche, St Louis 130–1
Brittin, Matt *167*, *251*
Bromenschenkel family 48–9, *49*
Broughton, Keith 110, *237*
Broughton, Mel 127, *168*, *205*, *225*, *251*
Broughton, Paddy 15, 26, 29, *30–1*, 35, *39*,
    46, *46–7*, *50*, 51, 52, 55, 59, 63, 64, *64*,

65, *70–1*, *73*, *77*, *85*, 86, *91*, 95, 96, *98*,
104, *105*, *110*, *111*, 112, *112*, 114, *119*,
122, 127, 130, *130*, *132*, 135, *135*, 137,
140–1, 142, *150–1*, *153*, *155*, *156*, 165,
167, 176, 192, 198, 200, *202*, 204, 208,
213, *217*, 220, *225*, 230, *234–5*, 236,
236–7, *238*, *239*, 243–4, 245, 247,
250, *251*
Browning, Robert 5
Brown, Michael 133

Cadillac John 186
Cambridge University Boat Club (CUBC) 104
Canadian Overseas Development office 248
Cancer Alley (chemical plants along
    Mississippi River between Baton Rouge
    and New Orleans) *208*, 209, *209*, 212–13,
    216–17
Cape Girardeau, Missouri 144, 146
chicken wings 56–7, 76, 142, 207
Chirrapah, Richmond 21, 22, 23, *22–3*, 79,
    80, 131, 249
Chmiel, Alison *167*, 196, *196*, *250*
Chmiel, Marysh *140–1*, *167*, 196, *196*, *197*,
    198–9, *250*
Church of the Latter-day Saints 115
Clarksdale, Mississippi 184–9, *184*, *186–7*,
    189, 190, *190*
Colborn, Carla *81*
Colling, Mike 126, *126–7*, *250*

Conty, Alex 51–2, *52*, 110, *110*, 114, 131,
    165, *165*, 179, 184, 200, *237*, *250*
cotton gin 192, *193*, 194
Cottonmouth/Pit Viper/Water Moccasin
    139–40
cotton trade 190–5, *190*, *191*, 192, *193*,
    194, 195
Country Inn, Deerwood 51
Courtmanche, Pat *81*

Dale, Jeremy 106, *210–11*, *212*, *250*
Davies, Dave 157–8
deer flies 50, *50–1*, 51
Deerwood, Minnesota 51, 56, 58
Doreen (boat) *15*, 86, *99*, *176–7*, *178–9*

Eagle's Nest sports bar, Keithsburg, Illinois
    111, *111*, 112

Freeman, Morgan 186

Gate, Chris *85*, *86–7*, *136*,
    251
Gate, Freddie 86, *86*, *250*
Ghana, Africa 20–1, *20–1*, *22–3*, 79–80,
    131, 249
Goodman, Kathy 99, 100
Graceland, Memphis 168, 170
Greenville, Mississippi 191,
    192

Ground Zero, Clarksdale 186, *186–7*
Grumman aluminium canoes 26, 60
Guthrie Theatre, Minneapolis 78, *78, 79*
Guttenberg, Iowa 106, 108

Hannibal, Missouri 122, *124, 125,* 126,
   157, 158
Holden, Simon 181, *181,* 225, 244,
   250
Horgan, Lucy 46, *46–7, 47*
Horgan, Matt *46–7, 250*
Hotchin, Simon 166, *166, 251*
Hughes, Jeff *64, 65, 73, 251*
Hurricane Katrina 243

Illinois 110–22, *111, 116–17, 119, 120–1,*
   144, 146
Iowa 22, 60, 106–7, *107,* 108
Iowa River 108, 110

Johnson, Robert 184–5

Karwoski & Courage 79
Keithsburg, Illinois 110–12, *111*
Kennedy, Sean *237*
Kentucky 144, 146
King, Martin Luther 170
Koss, Johann Olav 10, 11, *62–3, 62–3,*
   65, 68, *68, 69, 69, 72, 73, 76, 77, 78,*
   80–1, 251

La Cross, Wisconsin 104, *104–5*
Lake Bruin, Louisiana 194, 195
Lake Itasca, Minnesota 14, 26, 30, *30, 31,*
   32, 40, 144, *237*
Lake Pepin, Minnesota/Wisconsin 88, *88–9,*
   90–1, 92–3, 95, 96, 98
lake trees 154, *154*
Lake Winnibigoshish, Minnesota 46, *46,*
   47, 47
Lansing, Iowa 106
Larson King 79
Lazy Acres guest house, Keithsburg,
   Illinois 110–11
Lock Number 1, Mississippi
   68
Lorraine Motel, Memphis 170, *170–1*
Louisiana 14, 62, 126, 140, 156, 172, 176,
   180, 192–248, *193, 194–5, 201, 202, 206,*
   207, 208–9, 210, 11, 212–13, 214–15,
   216, 217, 218–19, 221, 222–3, 225,
   226–7, 228–9, 230–1, 232, 233, 234–5,
   236–7, 238–9, 240–1, 242

Mahoney, Chris *236*
Mayne, Derek 19, *213, 225, 238, 250*
McCarty, John *119,* 121
McDougall, Magenta *139,* 156, *164–5, 167,*
   168, 225, *238–9, 251*
Memphis Civil Rights Museum, Tennessee
   170, *170–1*

Memphis, Tennessee 142, 157, 161, 165,
   168–71, *168–9, 170–1,* 172, *172–3,* 176,
   184, 203
Minneapolis, Minnesota 62, 68, 76–84, *77,*
   78, 79, 80–1, 82–3, 126, 144
Minnesota 14, 30–97, *30–1, 32–3, 34, 35,*
   36, 37, 38, 39, 40–1, 42–3, 44–5, 46–7,
   48– 9, 50–1, 52–3, 54–5, 56–7, 59, 60, 61,
   62–3, 64, 65, 66–7, 68–9, 70–1, 72–3,
   77, 78, 79, 80–1, 82–3, 84–5, 86, 87, 88,
   89, 90–1, 92–3, 94, 95, 96–7, 106, 126,
   144, 171
Minnesota Boat Club 78, 80, *80, 82–3*
Mississippi, state of 184–91, *184, 186–7,*
   189, 190, 191, 192, 194
Mississippi Million challenge:
   aim of 14
   barge traffic and 26, 106, 137, *160–1,*
      162–3, 165, 179, 188, 209, *209,* 13,
      217, 245
   birth/origin of journey 10–11, 14–15, 20–3
   boats (Richmond and Doreen)
      beauty of 86
      carrying *155*
      construction of *16–17*
      damage to and repair of 196, 197,
         197–8, 198
      launching of *30*
      preparation of *15*
      purchase of 86

completion of 224, *225*, *226*, *227*, 230–2, *231*, 232, *232*, *233*, 244

diet and nutrition 58, 200, 204, 206–7, *206–7*

difficulties encountered, array of 16–17

exit point from Mississippi River 243–4

fatigue and 69, *110*, 130, 200, *201*, 203, 206, 243, 244, 247

guest participants/rowers 26, 30, 104, 108, 161, 208 *see also individual participant name*

halfway point 114, 126, 130, *130*, 144

headwinds and 17, 19, 58, 62, 63, 69, 104, 106, 112, 127, 137, 142, 161–2, *161*, 165, 166, *166*, 179, 184, 188, 199, 203

'hitting the wall' 58, 206

injuries suffered 15–16, *51*, 114, *157*, 200, 203, 246

launch of skiffs on Lake Itasca 30, *30*

launch party *18*, 19, *19*

length/distances of rowing days, calculations of 142, 161, 176, 179

mantra, project 19

map of journey *9*

money raised 248–9

mosquitos and 16, 48, 50, 51, 157, 249

100–mile Mark 46, 47

$1 million dollar target 10, 11, 22, 79, 248

1,000 mile mark 122, 126, 144

party at completion of 236–7, *236–7*, *238–9*, 244, 245, 247–8

pivotal moments 144

planning 22, 26, 30, 62, 86, 161, 176, 246

presentation boxes 196

psychological challenges 156–8

rainfall and 34, 51, 69, 112, 114, 126, 130, 159, *159*, 160

receptions in support of 78, 79, 80, *80*

return home from 243

South, crossing into 144, 146, 148, 152–3, 190

support vehicles 26, *204*

thunderstorms and 112

tornados and 34, 176, 191

training for 156–7

2,000 mile mark 200

support team 48, 49, 51–2, 121, 216, 243, 246 *see also individual support team member name*

wildlife encountered 16, 34–5, 40, *40–1*, *42–3*, *45*, 95, *94*, 95, 99, *121*, 137–8, *138*, 140, *141*

Mississippi River:

accents along the 144, 146, 148, 152, 153

beauty of 34, 40, *40–1*, *44*, 45, 50, 56, *97*, *194–5*

characters/eccentrics along the 60–1, *60–1*, 114–15

dams on 30, 58, 62, 63, 88, 99, 106, 160, 220

dangers of 16–17 *see also individual danger name*

food and drink along the 49, *49*, 79, 56–7, 72, 76, 78, 118, 122, 134, 135, *134– 5*,

142, 144, 148, 150–1, 186, 204, 206–7, *206–7*, 220, 236

headwinds on 17, 19, 58, 62, 63, 69, 104, 106, 112, 127, 137, 142, 161–2, *161*, 165, 166, *166*, 179, 184, 188, 199, 203

locks on 68, 69, *69*, 72, 126, 130, *131*, 144, 155, 160, 220

power of 45

racism along the 170–2

rapids on 31, 34, 45, 58–9, 60, 63, *64*, 198

shape of *27*, *37*, 56

size/scale of 26, *96–7*

slavery along the 170, 172, 185, 190–1, 192

source 32, *32*

wildlife on 16, 34–5, 40, *40–1*, *42–3*, *45*, 95, *94*, 95, 99, *121*, 137–8, *138*, 140, *141*

Missouri 68, 122–7, *124*, *125*, 130–5, *130–1*, *132–3*, *134*, *135*, 137, 144, 146, 157, 158, 190

Missouri Moonshine 158, *158*

Missouri River 26, 130

mosquitos 16–17, 48, 50, 51, 157

Muddy Waters 186

Mulcahy, Graeme *28*, *29*, 63, *63*, 65, *70–1*, *81*, *89*, *98–9*, *100*, 108, 109, *109*, *132*, 133, *133*, 142, *150–1*, 161, 186, 198, 220

Murphy, Niall 131

Natchez riverboat, New Orleans *222–3*

Nauvoo, Illinois 115, 118, 119, *119,*
    120–1
New Orleans, Louisiana 14, 62, 126, 156,
    172, 176, 200, 208, *216, 217, 218–19,*
    220, *221, 222–3, 236, 236–7, 238–9,*
    240–1, 242, 243, 244, 247

Oxford and Cambridge Boat Race 104

Pappy's Smokehouse, St Louis 134, *134–5*
Phillips, Cooee 104
Phillips, Jim 192
Pier 4 Café and Smokehouse, Alma 100
Presley, Elvis 170
Pritchard, Charlie 20, *20,* 21, *34, 54–5, 77,*
    131–2, 179, 203, *234, 250*

Quincy Boat Club, Quincy, Illinois 122

racism 170–2
radar reflectors 144, *147*
Raspberry Island, Minnesota 79
Razorblade (local blues legend) 186, 188
Red Stick 212, 213
Red's Lounge, Clarksdale 185–6, *186*
Red Wing, Minnesota 95–6, *95*
Rees, Jerry *236, 250*
Richard and Don (kayakers) 144, 146,
    146
Richmond (boat) *2, 12–13, 15,* 22, 86, *99,*
    176–7, 178–9, 198, *198*
Right To Play (RTP) 10, 11, 20–1, *20, 21,* 22,
    26, 62, 78, 79, 244, 248–9

St Paul Yacht Club, Minnesota 76, 84
Sam Adams beer 56–7, 72, 76, 135, 142,
    207, 220, 236
Sayers, Gavin 205, *205, 251*
Schroeder, Pamela 84, *85, 250*
Shakespeare, William: *Henry V* 224
61 Highway *185*
slavery 170, 172, 185, 190–1, 192
Smith, Joseph 115
snakes, water 16, 17, 139–40
Stanley and Thomas *16–17*
St Louis Cardinals 132, *132, 133*
St Louis, Missouri 68, 126–7, 130–5, *132,*
    133, 134, 135, 137, 144, 146, 158,
    160
St Paul, Minnesota 68, 72, 76

Target 79
Taylor, John 114, *119, 250*
Tennessee 142, 157, 161, 165, 168–73,
    168–9, 170–1, 172–3, 176, 184, 203
Thornton, James Oscar 192
Three Kings Special School, Ghana 249
Twinn, Alf 104

Upper and Lower St Anthony's Falls lock,
    Mississippi 68, 72
Upper Mississippi River and Illinois
    Waterway 9-Foot Channel Project 68

Van Wassenhove, Ewaut 60–1, *60–1,* 114,
    115
Vickers, Mark *54–5, 251*

waffles with chicken 76, 78
Walsh, Patrick *238*
Wapello, Iowa 108, 110
Webber, Steve 113, *113, 251*
Webster, Freddie 134
Weevil, Boll 192, 230
Whitney, Eli 194
Whitworth, James 130, *130, 251*
Williamson, Harry 30, 31, *30–1, 250, 251*
Williamson, Julie 20, 22–3, 30, 32, 34, *34,*
    48, 62, 80, 88, 127, 132, *132, 168,* 195,
    203, *233, 234, 238–9,* 243, 247, *251*
Wilson, Mark 30, *30–1, 38, 39, 250*
Wisconsin 98–105, *98–9, 100–1, 102–3,*
    104–5
Woods, Simon 139, *139, 164–5, 250*

Zaleski, Carin 80, *80, 239, 242*
Zeronian, Sarkis 161–2, *161,* 165, *250*

Picture Credits

All pictures © Jeremy Dale except for the following:

Matt Brittin: p167 (top),180, 198, 199

Paddy & Mel Broughton: p36, 37, 38, 39, 46, 50, 51, 59, 112, 113, 118, 120, 132, 133, 134, 135, 136, 138, 139, 140, 141, 154, 155, 156, 157, 158, 159, 161, 162, 163, 164, 165, 166, 167 (bottom), 176, 194

Kelly Ennis: p1

Charlie Green: p143, 184, 189

Kate Hampton p122, 123, 124, 125, 131, 144, 147, 160

Laura Mosedale: p47

Mark Vickers: p12, 13, 40, 41, 45, 48, 49, 52, 53, 66, 67, 70, 71, 150, 151

Julie Williamson: p15, 18, 20, 21, 22, 23, 28, 29, 30, 31, 32, 33, 34, 35

© Shutterstock: p4, 6, 10, 24, 44, 56, 74, 97, 116, 128, 170, 171, 173, 174, 240, 246, back endpaper

© iStock: back cover, front endpaper

First published in 2018 by Napier Publishing

ISBN 978-1911195948

Printed and bound by LEGO in Italy.